A Story Is a Promise

A Story
Is a
Promise

Good Things to Know Before You Write
that Screenplay, Novel, or Play

Bill Johnson

Blue Haven Publishing • Portland, Oregon

Printed and bound in the United States of America.

Published by
Blue Haven Publishing
Collins View Performance Center
318 SW Palatine Hill Rd.
Portland, OR   97219

Book Design: Bill Johnson
Cover Design: Bill Johnson
Photo: Jack Sanders

Second Edition.
10 9 8 7 6 5 4 3 2 1

ISBN 0-9673932-0-5

PUBLISHER'S CATALOGING-IN-PUBLICATION DATA

Johnson, Bill
    A Story Is a Promise / by
        Bill Johnson — 2nd ed.
        p.   cm.
        Includes bibliographical references and index.
        ISBN 0-96783932-0-5
        1. How-to 2. Story Writing
        I. Title

Dedication

This book is dedicated to

> Paramahansa Yogananda,
> who taught me how to find freedom,
> joy, and peace in life.

> And

> Doctor Gary Solomon,
> who helped me figure out
> how to live in this world.

Introduction

This book is designed to guide writers toward a new understanding of the process of creating and writing dramatic stories.

Section One explores…

>How a story functions like a promise
>How to fulfill a story's promise to its audience

Section Two explores how a story's elements are designed, including…

>Techniques to create a story premise
>Developing dynamic characters
>How to create a plot
>Understanding what's at stake in your story
>The role of ideas in stories
>The role of conflict in storytelling

Section Three offers essays that explore how to outline a story, including…

>Examples of story lines and plot lines
>Story Director™, a unique outline process

Section Four offers tips on how to begin a story, including…

>Creating a dramatic first sentence
>Writing with a free voice

Section Five explores principles of storytelling through reviews of popular novels, screenplays, and plays.

Foreword

Twenty-eight years making short films had convinced me I was well prepared to write a screenplay or a novel. I'd written, produced, and directed almost a hundred films for theatrical release, television, corporate presentations, documentaries, and education, receiving forty-four awards and a grant from the American Film Institute. Yet, as I struggled to write my first novel, I soon floundered and found myself lost in a maze without a map. What I hadn't grasped was how great the leap from a short film to a novel or feature length script.

I began to read everything I could find on writing novels and screenplays, nearly eighty books altogether. Each focused on pieces of the larger picture, not the whole. All were filtered through the author's own unique perspective, each different enough from the others to create confusion. They wrote as though the essential principals of dramatic writing were too vast for anyone to cover in a single book. However, a handful did come close enough to convince me it was possible. I also had this nagging feeling there was a higher level to storytelling that none of them were discussing, and I sensed that if I didn't understand that, I wasn't going anywhere.

One night in March, 1995, while searching the Writer's Forum on AOL, I came across a series of postings that got my attention. They began, "I would like to open a discussion into story movement, what it is, and how to create it." I read them all, then read them again. Nothing I'd come across before had so clearly cut to the very essence of how to tell a story. Here was someone who understood that higher level for which I aspired and who knew how to teach it.

Though I'd never met him, I offered my help as an editor. Perhaps I could be a sounding board for his ideas, someone to raise questions. I was pleasantly surprised when he responded to my email by accepting my offer. It was the start of a lasting friendship that began my own journey into the heart of storytelling. It would change my writing life forever.

I'd read many a story but never fully understood what was behind the "paint on the walls." It was clear that stories worked, but why did the writer choose a particular plot, or set of characters, or locale, or the individual words on the page for that matter? The beauty of what Bill does is contained in the series of steps he led me through, each building on the previous one, until I could see those principals in action in a story I was writing. He even taught me how to go about choosing the right dramatic words—no small feat. For the first time, things began to make sense and my writing began to steadily improve.

As time went by, Bill's personalized style of teaching was an inspiration. I was struck by the fact that this book was written in the same conversational style, one on one, as though Bill were talking to me, anticipating my questions, even raising issues that stimulated my thinking about the story I was writing, or one that I planned to write. It was clear that from his years of teaching experience that he could anticipate the kinds of questions I might ask, and even anticipate why I asked them. I came to realize that Bill has a unique understanding of what a writer needs to know to become a storyteller, and all of that is reflected in this book.

Now, whenever I'm in the midst of writing a story and am uncertain about where it's going or how to get there, this is the book I return to time and again for answers and inspiration.

Lawrence Booth

Acknowledgments

This book owes a debt to…

Lawrence Booth, founder of the Half Moon Bay Film School. His editorial assistance, probing questions, and friendship helped bring this book into being.

Tom Shaw, of Tom Shaw Productions. A filmmaker who generously helped others. Tom gave me a place to stay in his studio for a year to support the creation of the essays in this book. He was a true friend.

David Morgan, who introduced me to story analysis. David is a friend and mentor, and the country's finest story analyst.

Bill Snowden, whose friendship and support helped give me direction.

Elizabeth Lyon, who introduced the ideas in this book to many people.

Lynn Bey-Roode, who offered many insightful editorial suggestions.

Rebecca Black, who told me it was time to get started.

Contents

SECTION ONE

A STORY IS A PROMISE

Understanding the Human Need for Stories

Since prehistoric times, when our ancestors gathered around fires in caves, storytellers have been aware of how arranging events in a story-like fashion engages and satisfies audiences. This chapter explores how a well-told story satisfies an audience.

In the Beginning Is the Story

Coming into this world, we have needs for food and shelter. When those immediate survival needs are met, others come to the surface.

One is a need for acknowledgment. Yet, from the time we are born, how we are acknowledged shapes our expectations of what we can expect from life. From our families, we might take in the idea that we have worth. Or, that we don't. That we're destined to be a success in life. That we're destined to fail.

While we're digesting these ideas, we're also interpreting our experiences in life and developing our own sense of who we are. A sense of the meaning and purpose of our lives. A sense of how we fit in and what we deserve from life. A sense of how we matter to ourselves and to others.[1]

While we integrate our sense of who we are, our cultures suggest something about our place in the world. For example, if we're American, we love freedom. If we're French, we're romantic. If we're Italian, we're hot-blooded. If we're German, we're cold and unemotional. If we're blonde, we have more fun and are more desirable. We might enjoy having a particular kind of "mattering" bestowed on us by our culture. Or, we might enjoy rebelling against an external definition of who we are.

All of these cultural definitions are stories. To the degree we accept them or are forced to deal with others who believe them, these stories have an impact on

2

our lives and our sense of place in the world. Take away a person's sense of place or sense of belonging in the world, and you'll have an unhappy person.

Unfortunately, life doesn't revolve around ensuring that we feel we matter. That we fit in. That our lives have a meaning and purpose that is desirable to us. Even worse, life is often unpredictable. Events happen, but to no clear purpose. We get things from life—relationships, jobs, recognition—but not always what we want. Or, what we want goes to someone else. How do we deal with this?

Because people are inventive and creative, we make do. One way we make do is to tell ourselves stories that fulfill our needs. For example, regardless of the outward appearances and realities of our lives, we are heroic. We have honor. We are brave. Or we're fearful—but we have good reason to be. And God loves us. Or hates us and has cursed us, if that's our story need.

Because life can operate to remind us we *aren't* heroic or courageous, or whatever need to matter we desire to have validated, stories provide the shortest path for many people to have their needs to matter fulfilled.

If we feel life is unjust, we can experience in stories a place where justice prevails. A place where redemption can be dramatically won, if our lives lack hope of redemption (or worse, if our redemption is out of our control). A place in which we can imagine ourselves courageously exploring new worlds, even if we're too shy to say "hello" to our neighbors. Where our senses can be enlivened through thrilling experiences, albeit from a safe distance. Where true love conquers all. Where difficult issues can be examined in ways we find stimulating. Where mysteries are resolved. Where good defeats evil. Where evil defeats good, and we get to sit a book down or leave a movie theatre having survived the experience.

That's why issues such as courage, redemption, renewal, love, and honor are most often at the hearts of stories. A well-told story is an arrangement of words and images that re-creates life-like characters, issues, ideas, and events in a way that promises dramatic fulfillment of our needs, and then delivers on that promise.

A story, then, is a promise.

A story that clearly communicates its promise draws in an audience. Stories that fail to suggest their promise struggle to engage interest because people gravitate toward stories that promise to meet their particular needs.

A well-designed story, then, is a vehicle that transports its audience to a resolution of human needs that is satisfying and fulfilling. When we find a particular story journey to be dramatically potent and pleasing—one that promises to move us through desirable states of feelings, perceptions, or thoughts in a way that is more "true" than life (or life as we wish it to be)—we desire to re-experience the same story journey again and again.

Knowing what needs a story promises to fulfill for its audience creates the beginning of a foundation for understanding the craft of storytelling. Learning that craft is at the very heart of the art of storytelling.[2]

Which raises the question: how do you set out a story's promise?

That's answered in the next chapter.

Chapter Questions

What needs do stories fulfill in your life?

How are the stories you tell yourself about who you are different from your experiences in life?

What needs do the stories you create promise to fulfill for others?

What kind of stories about who you are as a person have been assigned to you by your cultural background? Your income level? Your level of education? Your family background?

Do the stories you most enjoy validate your choices in life? Or, do they help you to believe that under different circumstances, you would be a different person?

A Story Is a Promise

Perceiving that a story is a promise is a cornerstone of the foundation for understanding the art of storytelling. This chapter takes a closer look at how a story functions as a promise.

A story sets out its promise by offering details of life-like characters, issues, events, and circumstances, then editing and arranging those details to move an audience toward a desirable experience of resolution. For example, when a story created around the issue of courage fulfills its promise, the story's audience experiences a fulfilling state of courage. The story's audience experiences the truth of the story's promise.

Popular stories are often designed to revolve around a promise of some human need being acted out to dramatic fulfillment. The film *Rocky*[3], written by Sylvester Stallone (who also stars as Rocky), promises to be a story about self-respect. *The Wizard of Oz*[4], by L. Frank Baum, promises to be about Dorothy's dramatic journey to a new sense of who she is and the fulfillment of her need to belong. *Romeo and Juliet*, by William Shakespeare, promises to be a story about tragic love.

This focus on shaping the events and details of a story to a particular purpose makes a well-told story fundamentally unlike the vagaries of real life. The "true" facts of life generally don't arrange themselves to promise a story-like resolution and fulfillment. If they did, a factual account of the suicides of two teenagers distraught that their parents kept them apart would create the effect of the story *Romeo and Juliet*. The two versions are clearly not the same in mood, tone, or dramatic purpose.[5] The fact that two teens committed suicide is simply information. It's an account of an event. Assembling details of such an event doesn't create a story. The *truth* of a *story* like *Romeo and Juliet* leads us to deeply feel the nature of powerful love.

Often, a story's promise is set out through the introduction of characters designed to act out to resolution some clearly established issue of human need.

5

As the characters act to fulfill a story's promise, a story's audience comes to feel that the characters ring true and are "life-like." Characters in well-told stories should, more correctly, be called story-like, because it is through their actions revolving around a discernible dramatic purpose that a story's audience chooses to identify with a story's characters. By internalizing a story's journey to resolution via the actions of its characters, an audience experiences a dramatic journey toward the fulfillment of a particular story's promise, and the powerful resolution of unresolved feelings and beliefs of the audience around a particular story's issue of human need.

By editing away all the details not "true" to this journey, a storyteller creates a story that becomes all the more "real" and potent to an audience. Characters in stories about courage often perform impossible feats, not because it's humanly possible, but because a story's audience demands that the actions of the story's characters be story-like. That's why characters not created around a clearly defined dramatic purpose can appear to be lifeless, cardboard cutouts; such descriptions are often journalistic, accounts of who characters are. It doesn't matter how carefully they are described or how true the journalistic details of their description. A carefully described character who acts to no discernible dramatic purpose in a story can appear to be a lie, which leads a story's audience to turn away, just as we in real life turn away from those who lie to us about their promises.

A story, then, is not created by assembling details that are realistic or true to life; it is created by assembling details that have a dramatic purpose that resonates with an audience. Details that are story-like in their design and intent. That evoke the world of a story in a dramatically engaging way.

The same logic applied to understanding a character's role in fulfilling a story's promise applies to deciding what details of a story's environment the storyteller should describe. Only those details that revolve around making potent a story's promise in a way that makes a story's world ring true should be included. Environmental details that do not revolve around dramatically setting out a story's promise come across as lies or as having no purpose.

When writers create characters, events, and descriptive details that dramatically act out to fulfillment a story's promise, such writing is innately satisfying. The romantic can read novels that fulfill a need for romance. The lover of action, the need for heroic quests. The lover of literary fiction, stories that explore the human condition.

That's why there's a story for every need, even needs we didn't know we had until a storyteller draws us in to experience a particular story's world. As long as people desire to have their curiosity satisfied, their questions about life and existence explained and answered, their issues of human need validated, there will be a desire for stories.

That's why a story must promise something to its audience. For the writer to promise nothing is to violate the unwritten contract of a storyteller with his or her audience: that the story transport its audience to a satisfying, fulfilling resolution.

How a storyteller suggests a story's promise is set out in the following chapter.

Chapter Questions

What does your story promise its audience?

How do you introduce your story's promise?

What events fulfill your story's promise?

What is the promise of your life story? How does that impact the kinds of stories you enjoy?

What details evoke the drama of your story's promise?

Naming Your Promise

A story's opening scenes are vital. If they don't suggest a story's promise, that story risks either not fully engaging or losing its audience. How does one set out a story's promise? It's done by a process I call *naming*.

For example, *Rocky* is a story about self-respect. When the storyteller arranges for Rocky to be called a "bum" and thrown out of the gym where he trains, the story acts out Rocky's self-respect being actively undermined. That cues in the audience that the story is about self-respect. It *names* the story's promise.

By raising the issue as a question—can Rocky gain self-respect?—the story begins in an active voice. When an audience hears questions arising out of issues of human need, it naturally feels engaged over a story's course and outcome. The opening scenes of *Rocky*—or any well-told story—revolve around more than the introduction of a story's characters or plot, or an account of a character's life and situation. They operate around *naming* a story's promise in a dramatic way, i.e., in a way an audience is enlisted to care how a story will turn out. When a story's promise is clearly named, then blocked from resolution, the tension over a story's course and outcome can be transferred from a story's characters to its audience. When this tension is internalized by a story's audience, that audience is compelled to experience a story's resolution to relieve the tension created by the storyteller. I call this narrative tension.

One can see this process in the film *The Usual Suspects*[6], written by Christopher McQuarrie. The character Verbal refers to the men in a lineup—the usual suspects—as being men who would not be broken. That names the issue at the heart of the story: the power of will. It also presents the issue as a dramatic question. Could these men be broken? The dramatic answer is yes—by someone with a more powerful will. Getting to the dramatic answer of who that is draws viewers to the end of the film.

The events that begin *The Usual Suspects* also operate to suggest the story's

8

promise. One man interrupts another man's attempt to set a fire that will destroy a ship. When the second man, Keyser, is through with Keaton, the man who was trying to set the fire, he takes Keaton's life. These events *name* the story—by introducing two men engaged in a contest of wills—while raising the questions, what happened on this ship and who are these men? In answering these questions, the story's audience is drawn into the story's world and the resolution of its promise.

To better understand this process of *naming,* imagine someone showing you a childhood photograph. The physical frame around the photograph encloses the world the photograph sets out in much the same way a storyteller sets out a story's world within the frame of a novel, play, or film. Now you're told that one of the children in the school photo just inherited a million dollars and wants to donate the money to charity, but needs help making decisions. That suggests a particular plot. It only *suggests* a plot because it implies some events might happen, but that in itself is not a story. It is not a story because there is no promise to resolve some issue of human need. Writing about the inheritance would just be an account of a particular situation.

Now you're told that another child in the photo is the secret son of Adolph Hitler. That suggests another plot. A far-fetched one, but it serves my purpose of making a point. This new character only suggests a plot because there's no indication of any kind of story revolving around that character or any sequence of actions, just a question of what this character will do.

Now your friend tells you that he or she found true love with someone in the photo. That *names* the story. We now know it's going to be a story about true love. Such a story could conceivably have Adolph's son and the new millionaire as characters, as long as they have clearly identified dramatic purposes and then act to resolve issues arising from the story's promise.

What often leads storytellers down the path of failing to *name* their stories is their focus on presenting what is visual and apparent, using details to describe characters, actions, and a scene's environment. Unless the storyteller *names* the dramatic purpose that underlies these events and suggests a need for resolution of the deeper issue at play in them, all that other work is dramatically inert; it is an account that simply makes statements about static things. It's true that some accounts, a history of a civil war battle, for example, will satisfy a particular audience. An account of that battle is not the same as a story about some of the characters involved, however.

For example, to say that "John is five foot eight, one hundred thirty-eight pounds, blond, blue-eyed" might be true, but it fails to *name* a story issue around John. To say, however, that "John thought he knew what loneliness was, until he met Mary," *names* a story that John will act out, one about loneliness.

The above example is obvious, but that's better than being obscure in a way that suggests no dramatic purpose for a story's characters. Once writers learn how to clearly suggest a dramatic purpose, they can then learn how to be suggestive and less obvious. To help writers make a distinction between being dramatically obvious, obscure, or suggestive, I've created a scale that runs from zero to ten (see diagram next page). Zero represents obscure, five, obvious, ten, suggestive. Starting with what is dramatically obvious about a character can be a starting point toward being dramatically suggestive, and moving away from being obscure. To avoid being obvious, most struggling writers move toward being obscure, which often reduces a story to an account of what characters are doing.

"My name is Rocky" is obscure, a zero. "My name is Rocky and I'm a nobody and I want to be a somebody," is obvious. Rocky winning the bloody fight that opens the movie and his 'winnings' not being enough to buy a post-fight hamburger, and his reaction to that, is suggestive.

Some writers understand their story's promise but they overlay it with so many static descriptions of characters and events they obscure it. In a story's opening scenes, any character action, scene description, plot event, or character dialogue not arising from a story's promise and suggesting a need for its dramatic advance toward resolution risks having no clear meaning. When a storyteller communicates his or her story's promise and dramatic purpose, however, he or she can naturally reveal the motivations of their characters as they react to resolving the story's issues and events. A story's details then serve a purpose. To offer details that serve no purpose is comparable to trying to study facts for a test, without knowing the subject of the test. It's a situation that quickly becomes frustrating for an audience. The quickest way to deal with that frustration is to stop reading, or go see a different movie or play.

The quicker the storyteller communicates the role of characters and a story's events in fulfilling a story's promise, the more quickly an audience will desire to enter a story's world to experience its promise played out to resolution and fulfillment.

To be able to set a story's promise in an active voice, the storyteller needs to make a distinction between a story, its plot, characters, environment, and ideas.

(continued on page 12)

Being Dramatically Suggestive About a Character

To avoid being obvious, many struggling writers become obscure, writing sentences that offer details about characters instead of offering dramatic suggestions about characters that will draw an audience deeper into a story's world. To help writers create suggestive characters, I use the diagram below. I ask that writers start with an obvious statement about what's at stake for a character in a story. I then ask that the writer to create an obscure sentence that suggests nothing about what's 'true' for a character, then a sentence that is dramatically suggestive. The following example is from the novel Prince of Tides[7], by Pat Conroy.

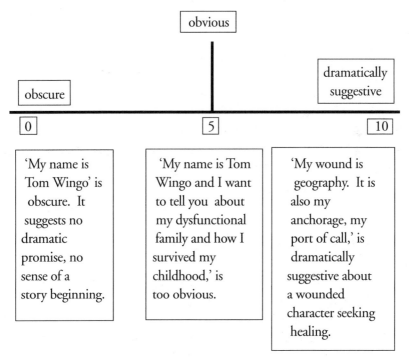

obscure	obvious	dramatically suggestive
0	5	10
'My name is Tom Wingo' is obscure. It suggests no dramatic promise, no sense of a story beginning.	'My name is Tom Wingo and I want to tell you about my dysfunctional family and how I survived my childhood,' is too obvious.	'My wound is geography. It is also my anchorage, my port of call,' is dramatically suggestive about a wounded character seeking healing.

When you introduce a character or create an opening event of a story, chapter or scene, consider whether you are being dramatically suggestive, obvious, or obscure.

In a story about courage, the story's *plot* is the action that make the story about courage dramatic. The *characters* in a story about courage will have issues of courage to resolve. The story's *environment* would be the places in which the story unfolds that would also potentially act as obstacles to a story's characters and challenge their courage. For example, in a story set on a mountain, the mountain itself could test the courage of the story's characters. In this story set on a mountain, the storyteller might explore *ideas* about courage, such as whether it's better to fight a losing battle with courage or to avoid the battle and stay alive.

Each of these story elements needs to be *named*—whether directly, indirectly, as a metaphor, etc.—in a way that suggests its dramatic purpose clear, without being obscure, or too obvious. If a scene merely highlights the actions of a story's characters but the dramatic purpose of those actions is unclear, it inherently risks failing to resonate with the story's audience. On occasion I read manuscripts that are deliberately obscure. These kinds of stories are sometimes written to satisfy the story's main audience, either the story's author, or a small audience educated about the story's subtle terrain. These kind of stories can work well as long as they satisfy their intended audience.

When a storyteller understands that a story's opening scenes revolve around setting out a story's promise, he or she has a guide to how to write such dramatically suggestive scenes.

The next chapter of the book offers examples of how to set out a story's promise.

Chapter Questions

What kind of events or actions or dialogue *names* your story's promise in its opening scenes?

What did you do to create drama around the introduction of your story's promise?

How do the actions of your main characters revolve around resolving your story's promise?

How do the events of your story highlight your story's promise?

Sustaining a Story's Promise

You now understand what needs your story promises to fulfill for your intended audience. You understand how to *name* your story's promise in a clear, discernible way. This chapter offers an overview of how a storyteller sustains a story's promise over the course of a story.

The process of sustaining a story's promise begins with an understanding of what drama is.

Drama is the anticipation of an outcome for an unresolved dramatic issue, character concern, story event, or idea.

You create an anticipation of a story's promise by suggesting that something around an issue such as courage, redemption, or renewal needs resolution. If you haven't set out that an issue, event, character goal, idea, etc, is in need of resolution, *there can be no drama over an outcome around it.* This holds true whether the issue is the outcome of a story's promise, the complications of a story's plot, the outcome of character actions, or the outcome of the issues and ideas a story raises. By interweaving the introduction of characters with issues to resolve that arise from a story's promise, a storyteller creates an anticipation of such characters moving the story toward the fulfillment of its promise.

For example, placing a character whose issue is gaining self-respect in an environment that denies him self-respect is the introduction to *Rocky*. What makes the story dramatic is that the only way Rocky comes to feel he can gain self-respect is to box Apollo Creed and remain standing at the end of the fight. I call that -- Rocky's need to prove that he's a somebody not a nobody - a dramatic truth. When characters both embody an issue of human need and are compelled to resolve that issue for internal or external reasons, they have a

13

dramatic truth to resolve. Characters who don't embody a dramatic truth are dramatically innert; they have nothing to resolve, no reason to act to shape events. Such characters risk being passive, simply reacting to events, instead of active, striving to shape a story's course or outcome.

An audience wants to feel a story's dramatic purpose is generating, scene by scene, experiences of resolution and fulfillment more potent and true than real life. More true because the edited arrangement of a story's elements is designed specifically to dramatically transport the audience toward a resolution of a story's promise. This is what makes stories so magical; it is their ability to transport audiences in a pleasurable manner. No movement, no magic.

To understand how a story transports an audience, consider *Romeo and Juliet*. It is a *story* about great love. Romeo's heartfelt, poetic longing for Rosalind introduces the issue of love. From out of the core dramatic issue of the story, the storyteller creates a *story line* composed of the events, dialogue, and actions that *name* what the story is about as it moves from its introduction to its fulfillment.

It is this quality of a story moving along its story line that makes a story satisfying to an audience. To not *name* and highlight a story's advance along its story line is to risk that a story fails to offer a compelling, dramatic journey to its audience. Worse, this lack of a story line suggests the storyteller is confusing an account of events with how to tell an engaging story.

That's why the members of an audience who are confused about a story's dramatic purpose generally aren't emotionally or thoughtfully engaged by the actions of its characters or plot. In effect, the storyteller races his or her characters and plot events in circles to create the effect of a story moving toward a dramatic destination. But, in reality, the audience realizes they aren't going anywhere. A good story is viceral in its ability to transport an audience. People feel moved or they don't. No movement, no story magic.

The most common mistake of inexperienced writers is not clearly establishing and sustaining their story's advance along its story line. This is ruthlessly damning. It creates a story that is a collection of meaningless details that suggest no promise or dramatic purpose, just as a collection of railroad cars sitting isolated on sections of disconnected tracks fails to suggest the possibility of a journey toward a destination. Offering more detailed descriptions of the railroad cars doesn't change that they sit motionless on disconnected tracks.

Just as a typical railroad train travels on two rails that compose a track, for a story to advance toward its resolution and fulfillment of its promise there needs to be a second "rail" to accompany the story line. That second rail is the *plot line.* When a story's characters act to overcome obstacles generated by a story's plot, their actions compose a story's plot line.

In *Romeo and Juliet*, for example, the *story* is about great love. Its plot is about the actions of the characters that act out this greatness. This story advances from its introduction along both a *story line* and a *plot line.* Together, they create the mechanism that allows for the story's audience to experience a discernible dramatic progression toward a story's resolution (plot) and fulfillment (story). Storytellers, in fact, create the plot obstacles their characters must overcome for the very purpose of making a story's progression along its story line dramatic. The catch is that those plot obstacles must arise from a story's dramatic purpose and promise in the same way the issues that compose and name its story line arise.

The issues characters bring to stories to resolve must also impact a story's events in a way that can be assigned meaning by the story's audience. How a story's characters respond to a story's plot events enable an audience to judge how far a story has advanced along its story line. The closer Romeo and Juliet come to proving their love, the closer the story is to its fulfillment, even if that fulfillment revolves around their deaths.

Many writers struggle with the issue of creating a story line that parallels their plot line because a story line only exists to the degree that the storyteller evokes it through the response of a story's characters to a story's events. Many struggling writers assume that characters + conflict + plot + resolution = story. Only, however, when a storyteller's story and plot elements interweave to create the effect of a dramatic progression toward fulfillment *and* resolution of issues of human need, or offer potent illuminations and revelations about life, does a story fully engage and reward the attention of an audience. Without that arrangement, character actions and plot events become merely a sequence of events that suggest no dramatic significance. They are an account of events and character actions.

Some writers so seamlessly weave together their plot and story lines that they appear joined. This could be compared to a magnetic train that runs on a single rail. The inexperienced writer trying to duplicate this process, however, must be careful that he or she is not simply overlaying personal feelings about a story's core dramatic truth onto plot events. If a storyteller's plot events fail to inspire or evoke feelings of fulfillment for an audience, such a story has failed to transport its audience in a desirable way. That's why stories that are merely sequences of action—this happened, then that happened—

can fail to emotionally or thoughtfully engage an audience. Such stories lack a discernible story line composed of events with resolutions evoking desirable perceptions, feelings, or epiphanies for the storyteller's audience. They fail to offer the release of narrative tension for the story's audience.

While some plot events can be designed to be so creative, shocking, nerve wracking, titillating, exciting, intriguing, or imbued with a grand sense of spectacle that they engage and reward the attention of an audience, more often when the events on a plot line becomes divorced from a story and its promise, they simply become life-like and inconsequential. They have a beginning, middle, and end, but no frame of reference as to what it is that they're a dramatic beginning, middle, and end *of.* I see examples of this in big-budget, special-effects driven Hollywood films that fail to satisfy an audience. Much spectacle, no heart, no story sense, no story magic.

The craft required to create multiple plot threads or time lines that evoke a story advancing along a single story line leads to the difficulties some inexperienced storytellers encounter when they try to create complex stories. If there's no unity of purpose at the heart of a story and its events, there's no common story line or plot line along which a story as an entity advances. The different story threads split apart into disconnected fragments of plot lines that don't move in a common direction. The audience senses that the different story elements aren't creating the purposeful, organized effect of a well-designed story. Often struggling storytellers compound this mistake by introducing more plot threads and characters to maintain some hold on the audience. Unfortunately, it only proves that the authors are unaware of why their stories aren't engaging. Recent, well-told film stories with mulitple time lines include *The Limey* and *Toto le Hero*.

Keep in mind that a simple story line for *Romeo and Juliet* could read: The beginning of the story line introduces a story about great love. The middle of the story line sets out the complications around this great love proving itself. The end of this story line is the fulfillment offered by this great love proving itself. There is a beginning, middle, and end.

A simple plot line for this story could read: The beginning of the plot line sets out events that introduce a story about great love. The middle of the plot line consists of events that escalate the drama around the outcome of whether this great love can prove itself. The end of this plot line is the resolution of the story that proves that great love can overcome all obstacles, even death. Again, a beginning, middle, and end. Simple movement. Complexity can be built and layered over this simplicity.

A story line is more than an occasional billboard alongside a plot line highway. It's an integral part of every aspect of a story.

If understanding the distinction between a story line and plot line is still difficult, think of a story and its plot as comparable to heat and flame. Heat is the tangible presence of flame, while flame is a concrete manifestation of heat. A story that generates no quality of heat also struggles to generate a visible manifestation of flame. It risks being a flame that generates no sensation of heat for its audience. An audience that comes to a story for the emotional, sensory, and intellectual heat it generates will turn away from a cold and lifeless story flame.

If you understand the difference between an account of an event and a story inspired by events, you're on the right path.

The ability to set out and sustain a story's promise in a way that dramatically and magically transports an audience is an important part of a foundation for understanding how to write dramatic stories.

In the next chapter, I'll explore how one demonstrates the ability to fulfill a story's promise.

Chapter Questions

Can you describe a story line for your story in simple terms and in three sentences?

Can you describe your plot line using three sentences?

Was your first attempt to write a story line and plot line obvious and clumsy? Good! If it's visible to you, it should be visible to your audience. Once you learn how to clearly set out your story line and plot line, you can work on creating dramatic beginnings for your stories that are suggestive and dramatic, without being too obvious or too obscure.

How to Make a Down Payment on Your Promise

If a story is a promise, how does the storyteller demonstrate to an audience his or her ability to fulfill a story's promise? By making a down payment on it. That communicates an ability to *pay off* on the story's larger promise, just as someone making a payment on a debt suggests an ability to pay off the whole debt.

How does one make this down payment?

The Usual Suspects opens on Keaton, a survivor of great carnage on a ship. Keaton is ready to destroy himself in a fiery explosion. This makes clear that Keaton has a powerful will. But will he succeed? The dramatic answer to that question is that a man of even stronger will interrupts and won't let Keaton die yet. This man speaks to Keaton, and Keaton gives the other man a name, Keyser. They speak briefly, then Keyser kills Keaton and walks away. He reignites the flame Keaton began and makes a narrow escape from the explosion that consumes the ship. A dramatic entrance and exit, indeed.

This scene suggests the story will be about the power of will by showing this life and death contest of wills. That's how the story makes a *down payment* on its promise. It sets up a question within the initial scene revolving around the power of will, and dramatically answers the question. At the same time it sets up larger questions that will draw the audience through the story. Who is Keyser? What happened on the ship?

In the opening chapter of *The Hunt for Red October* [8], by Tom Clancy, Clancy sets up the question: will Ramius, the Commander of the *Red October*, be able to implement his plan to escape the oppression of Soviet communism? The dramatic answer is yes. While that provides a down payment on the story's promise, the "how" and "where to" of Ramius's intent to escape are left for future chapters.

In *Rocky*, an early question is: will Rocky find a way to convince a young girl that by hanging out on the street she's picking up the wrong kind of reputation? The dramatic answer is no. The girl recognizes Rocky is everything he's telling her not to be, a nobody hanging out on the streets. That sets up an even more powerful question: will Rocky be able to gain the self-respect he obviously thinks is valuable? Getting the answer to that question requires a journey to the story's dramatic destination.

Romeo and Juliet opens with a lethal brawl that raises the question, is Romeo safe? When Benvolio is sent to check on Romeo, he discovers that Romeo is love-sick for Rosalind. He advises Romeo to go someplace he can see other beauties, advice which Romeo rejects because of the depth of his feelings for Rosalind, but wanting to see Rosalind leads him to Juliet.

The Wizard of Oz opens with Dorothy trying to keep Toto safe from a neighbor. Trying to make sure Toto has a place where he belongs leads to Dorothy's adventure in Oz.

To test whether you're making a downpayment on your promise, use the zero-five-ten scale on page 11 to write out how you're making that down payment in a way that is obvious, then obscure, then suggestive. Let yourself be obvious, then obscure, then move into being suggestive. If you want to start with being suggestive and work back toward obvious and obscure, that's fine as well. The goal is to understand the difference.

Demonstrating an ability to make a down payment on a story's promise is another important aspect of creating a well-told story. How to sustain that promise throughout the course of a story is the focus of the next chapter.

Chapter Questions

How are you making a down payment on your story's promise in your opening scenes?

How does your initial down payment draw your audience deeper into your story?

How are you setting up a story question in your opening scenes so that it will draw your audience to the end of your story?

Writing Dramatic Moments

Just as a story engages the interest of an audience by introducing its promise in a dramatic way, the moments within a story's scenes can also create drama. To create that drama, moments in scenes can be designed to be emotionally or thoughtfully engaging, or illuminating of ideas that add depth to a story, or designed to offer fresh, vivid perceptions of a story's events.

To understand this process of writing dramatic moments, keep in mind that anticipation is the key to creating drama. To create anticipation, something must either be set into motion as a scene opens, or something must be presented as ripe with a sense of impending movement. To show this process in action, consider again *The Usual Suspects*. The opening scene introduces Keaton as a wounded man. Dead bodies close by suggest a recent battle. Keaton lights a cigarette, then ignites a line of fuel that leads toward some fuel tanks. We anticipate that the explosion and fire will kill him.

That's the introduction to this moment. Note how it's tied to the central issue of the story's promise—the power of will. Keaton is presented as a man of strong will, ready to take his own life. If the moment continued and the ship had blown up, the audience would have been left with simple questions. What happened on the ship? Who was the man who set the fire?

Before the line of flame sets off an explosion, someone urinates on the flame from above, extinguishing it. This develops more drama around the outcome of the initial moment. It takes the moment in a direction not expected. Because the scene was taken in an unexpected direction, the audience is given an answer to one question, will the line of flame set off an explosion? The answer is no. Which sets up a larger question: who is the man who put out the flame? Note how the dramatic shape and details of the moments of this scene draw us into desiring answers to this larger question.

With the attention of the audience drawn to the question of the identify of the second man, he joins the first man and asks, "How you doing, Keaton?" This

20

answers the question: who is the first man? At the same time, the sequence of action sets up other, larger questions. What was Keaton doing there? Was he trying to set off an explosion that would kill himself as well as the second man? Who is the second man? What starts out as a simple moment—will the line of fire set off an explosion?—continues to raise new questions. There is a process here of both setting up a moment with a potential outcome and then shaping that initial moment to have an unexpected twist that heightens its dramatic impact.

In that vein, the process of setting up questions and providing answers continues. Keaton gives an identity to the second man, the name Keyser. This gives a partial answer to the question, who is he? Note, however, that we don't see Keyser's face, and that sets up other questions. What does he look like? Why is his identity being withheld? To get those answers, we have to journey forward. That's the purpose of these moments, to draw the story's audience deeper into the story in an engaging way.

This same process can be applied to any moment in any scene. By each moment in a story having a dramatic question that sets up a desire for an answer, the storyteller creates moments that draw an audience through scenes.

This does not mean that every moment in the story must have a dramatic shape with a beginning, middle, and end. As *Suspects* continues, Verbal, the narrator, testifies before a grand jury and says, "It all started…" This is a promise to give us the answers to what happened on the ship. Once that purpose is met, the scene is over. The scene is only as long as it needs to be to fulfill its dramatic purpose.

What follows in the opening scenes of *The Usual Suspects* are the quick introduction to several characters. Todd Hockney works in a garage. As armed police rush into the garage and toward him with guns drawn, he calmly reaches for something. Will he be shot? Will he shoot someone? This moment demonstrates the power of his will. The other character introductions follow. Each introduction gives each character a distinctive personality while also suggesting how tough each man is. As an audience, we've been set up to expect something to come out of the powerful willfulness of these men.

The dramatic moments in *The Usual Suspects* generally revolve around action. Another storyteller telling a story about the power of will might create scenes that revolve around a process of illumination of ideas about the power of will. For example, Fellini's *8 1/2* dramatically presents a film director who is adrift in a sea of choices with no ability—no will—to make up his mind. It's a story that covers some of the same terrain but with an entirely different artistic purpose and outcome from *The Usual Suspects*. The storytelling process—how to set into motion a story via scenes that advance the story along its story and plot lines—is the same.

Struggling storytellers often damage their stories by simply presenting information about characters without creating dramatic moments that suggest anticipation of some outcome. To give us details about what Verbal and the others look like is not the same as setting a story into motion via their actions. Another dangerous path is filling scenes with details about the environment of a story. This risks creating scenes that collectively have no dramatic tension, no conflict over an outcome, no sense of dramatic purpose. Such moments are inert. A collection of non-dramatic moments creates a non-dramatic story.

To understand that a moment in a scene has a beginning, middle and end is to perceive that the outcome of a moment in a scene can be made dramatic and that its outcome can be unexpected to both a story's characters and a story's audience. That is what makes some stories so stimulating. Both the audience and the characters can never quite know, moment to moment, how things are going to turn out. Both the audience and the characters have to keep going deeper into the story to get answers. Heightened dramatic movement, great magic.

A storyteller who gives an audience no choice about having to find out how a story turns out, understands a vital aspect of the craft of storytelling.

Chapter Questions

How can you describe the beginning, middle, and end of a dramatic moment from the opening scene of your story?

What did you do to make the outcome of that opening moment dramatic?

What information did you offer in that moment that names your story's promise?

How does the dramatic outcome of your opening moment set your plot into motion?

Suggesting a Dramatic Truth

A story's characters embody dramatic truths when characters feel compelled to resolve issues of human need. Drama is an anticipation of an outcome. A character who embodies a dramatic truth suggests a character's purpose. A significant character who fails to embody a dramatic truth risks coming across as a collection of details, worse, purposeless details. Let me demonstrate.

"John was five foot eight, with blond hair, a senior in college, an avid chess player."

This collection of words makes a statement about John. It creates no sense of anticipation about John as a character, nor does it suggest an issue of human need that John feels compelled to resolve. A collection of similar statements in sequence would risk simply assembling details about John for an audience to try and understand. This quickly becomes frustrating, because there's nothing to assign meaning to all the details.

If I write, "John was lonely," that's still a statement about John, but in a story about loneliness, it serves to *name* the story. Still, it fails to create a sense of anticipation about what might arise from John's loneliness, or what might compel John to act to resolve his loneliness.

Writing, "A sense of loneliness radiated from John," makes John's state of emotion more vivid, but not more dramatic. It still creates no sense of drama over an outcome to what we know about John. But if I write, "John thought he understood the true depths and pain of loneliness until he met Mary," that creates a sense of anticipation, and that anticipation revolves around the issue of loneliness. Now a description of John's loneliness ties into John's dramatic truth. It is part of the beginning of a story about loneliness with characters named John and Mary, and it suggests that something about Mary has made John's loneliness untenable. It's an obvious beginning, but a beginning that could be revised to be more subtle or suggestive, artful or elusive. It's a starting point.

To avoid being obvious, many writers offer details about characters that are

23

obscure, that do not suggest a dramatic truth. I suggest writers be obvious about a character's dramatic truth as a way station toward writing that is dramatically suggestive. (Use diagram page 11 to suggest dramatic truths.)

Just as characters can embody a dramatic truth, a story's environment embodies a dramatic truth when it impacts a story's characters in a purposeful manner. For example, a lonely character might be put into a warm, loving environment that increases his or her loneliness. A character struggling to control his or her temper could be placed into an environment that is aggravating, sunlight too bright, noises too loud, etc. A recent movie, *Insomnia*, places a character who can't sleep into an environment where the sun never sets. Environments that fail to embody dramatic truths risk being passive details that fail to ring true because they lack a context within a story's truth.

Words that lack an active sense of purpose that revolves around a dramatic truth are passive. This holds true even if a writer is describing characters in action if no underlying story movement around resolution of a dramatic truth is created. When words revolve around a discernible dramatic purpose that advances a story, they can create a vivid, palpable sense of movement toward a story-like destination. Note the quality of dramatic truth suggested by these words from the opening of *Moby Dick*[9], by Herman Melville,

> Call me Ishmael. Some years ago—never mind how long precisely— having little or no money in my purse, and nothing particular to interest me on shore, I thought I would sail about a little and see the watery part of the world. It is a way I have of driving off the sphleen and regulating the circulation. Whenever I find myself growing grim about the mouth; when it is a damp, drizzly November in my soul; whenever I find myself involuntarily pausing before coffin warehouses, and bringing up the rear of every funeral I meet; and especially whenever my hypos get such an upper hand on me that it requires a strong moral principle to prevent me from deliberately stepping into the street, and methodically knocking people's hats off—then, I account it high time to get to the sea as soon as I can.

By introducing a man obsessed with this "November in my soul," a story about obsession is named. The storyteller also suggests Ismael's obsession has grown and threatens to take over his life. He is a ripe dramatic character, both physically and emotionally, because he is compelled to deal with his obsession.

The story deepens with the introduction of Ahab and his obsession that, unlike Ishmael's, will lead to the deaths of a number of others. The issue of obsession in this story evolves into a thoughtful story question. When does an obsession for a good cause become evil? That is one of the more compelling questions of the twentieth century, with the many millions who have died as a result of others' obsessions. It is one reason *Moby Dick* is acknowledged as a classic. Its author took a dramatic truth that spoke to future generations and wrote a compelling story that fulfilled its promise via rich, poetic language.

Great writers communicate great states of emotion and a need to act in a few words. In *Prince of Tides*, by Pat Conroy, the opening line is:

My wound is geography.

Conroy creates a sense of who the story's narrator is through taking a literal fact—that Tom Wingo is from Colleton, South Carolina—and overlaying it with a truth about Tom, that he is wounded.

The story question of *Prince of Tides* is:

Can Tom Wingo be healed?

That is the dramatic purpose of this story. In just one sentence, this writer captures not only a beginning of a portrait of a complex character, but he also sets out the novel's story question and begins the process of creating drama over the question of Tom's ability to find healing and resolve his dramatic truth. On a deeper level, the storyteller is asking if *any* of us can find healing for our wounds. That is why the story, with its answer to this question, is so emotionally and thoughtfully moving to its intended audience.

Catherine Ryan Hyde's *Funerals for Horses*[10] opens with this subtitle,

The God of Growing Up

This suggests a story about growing up. It also raises questions, who is the god of growing up? What led someone in the story to need such a god?

The opening lines of the novel,

My brother Simon was forty-two years old. I pray he still is.

This suggests a story about loss, and raises an immediate question, what happened to Simon? Continuing,

> I shame and cajole his family into believing with me, but their wicks have burned down, their flames left to flicker, like the light they pretend to leave on in the windows for Simon, like their own dwindling lives.

In a few graceful, beautifully written lines, Hyde suggests the dramatic truth of this family. She writes the truth about this family, that they aren't as concerned about Simon's disappearance as the narrator. The descriptive details about the family that come later will ring true because they have a context.

This following opening is from *A Confederacy of Dunces*[11], by John Kennedy O'Toole.

> A Green hunting cap squeezed the top of the fleshly balloon of a head.

This description speaks a truth about this character.

> The green earflaps, full of large ears and uncut hair and the fine bristles that grew in the ears themselves, stuck out on either side like turn signals indicating two directions at once.

Again, this is both description, and description that informs the audience about the nature of this character in a comic tone.

> Full, pursed lips protruded beneath the bushy black moustache and, at their corners, sank into the little folds filled with disapproval and potato chip crumbs.

This description suggests this character's outlook on the world, and, in return, suggests what the world thinks of this character.

The following opening from Dean Koonce's *From the Corner of His Eyes*[12] demonstrates how this author draws in an audience with a suggestion of a character's dramatic truth.

> Bartholomew Lampion was blinded at the age of three, when

surgeons reluctantly removed his eyes to save him from a fast-spreading cancer, but although eyeless, Barty regained his sight when he was thirteen.

This sentence immediately raises a compelling question: how does a boy without eyes regain his sight?

While there is no *one* right word for a story, there is a process that underlies how strongly some words suggest a story's dramatic truths. Storytellers like Jane Austen and William Faulkner are revered because of the masterful command and artistic craft they bring to creating characters that fully embody dramatic truths. Their fiction is never less than deeply realized truths.

To help writers create dramatic sentences, I have them use the zero-five-ten scale on page 11 and state in an obvious way the purpose of a sentence. For example, "John is angry." I then have them write a sentence about John's anger that is obscure, "John talked about the weather." Lastly, a sentence that is dramatically suggestives. "Life kept a half-step ahead of John, even in his dreams."

Some writers struggle because they overlay their feelings onto a sentence like, 'John talked about the weather.' To the author, this sentence has a subtext, because the author is aware of the story's promise and John's dramatic truth and narrative tension. For this kind of sentence to have a subtext of meaning for an audience, an underlying promise and truth must be accessible.

Storytelling that lacks this subtext often lacks the fuel that gives words and images that special power to transport an audience. For example, if a story's audience knows a character's principle issue is fear, and the storyteller writes a simple sentence about this character walking into a dark house, the audience understands the subtext. This is a character confronting fears rooted in other events. The context of the event also allows an audience involved or invested in this character to experience their own memories of fears and fearful experiences.

To discover whether you are creating sentences that suggest a subtext based on a character's dramatic truth, write a sentence about a character that is obvious, then obscure, then suggestive. Below each sentence, write what information your audience would need to understand a subtext. To understand how this works, consider the sentence diagram on page 11 with the example from Prince of Tides. The obscure sentence, 'My name is Tom Wingo,' suggests no subtext. The obvious sentence also Tom's dysfunctional family also lacks subtext; it's a statement about Tom. The third and actual opening sentence, 'My wound is geography. It is my anchorage, my port of call,' has a subtext that suggests loss, a connection to a place that is both broken and unbreakable, a sense that that which comforts the narrator also wounds him. That subtext creates a place in the story for the audience to be involved with the character and story. Consider that an obscure sentence is like fog, tiring to see through, easy to feel lost and frustrated. An obvious sentence is a hard surface a story's audience can only observe and would struggle to pass through into a story's world. A sentence with subtext has the depth that allows a story's audience to enter a story's world and share it with a story's characters.

Again, be clear about the subtext you bring to a sentence, and the subtext your intended audience will experience from what you've written.

Characters who don't embody a vibrant, clearly defined dramatic truth that needs to be resolved are dead. The longer you take to set out a character's dramatic truth, the longer you'll be dragging a corpse through your story. Generally getting a whiff of dead characters in a story's opening pages is enough for most readers.

If you know the dramatic truth of your life, are you creating characters who have the same intensity of energy around resolving their dramatic truths?

Play with creating dramatic, engaging sentences that suggest your character's dramatic truths and draw your audience forward to find out more. Don't be concerned with right or wrong, good or bad; just think about the dramatic truths you want to express, then think of a way to be suggestive about those truths while avoiding being obscure. If you can create one vibrant, suggestive sentence that vividly and potently suggests a dramatic truth, you're on your way to creating a story.

Chapter Questions

Can you write a sentence that makes a statement about a dramatic truth, and then rewrite it as a sentence that creates an anticipation of a potential outcome for that truth?

Can you write a sentence about a character that sets up an anticipation of an outcome for an issue such as courage, self-respect, or gaining understanding?

Do you know the dramatic truth of your life? Are you comfortable with the choices you've made to resolve your dramatic truth?

SECTION TWO

DESIGNING THE ELEMENTS OF YOUR STORIES

Premise—Understanding The Foundation of Your Story

Beginning a story in an active voice is a crucial aspect of storytelling. It suggests the ability of the storyteller to transport an audience to a story's dramatic destination. Creating a premise can be a great help toward understanding how to set in motion a story journey, and how to sustain that journey dramatically.

A story premise does three things. It sets out a story's core dramatic issue, it offers a description of the movement of that issue toward resolution, and it describes the fulfillment that resolution offers both a story's characters and its audience.

Dramatic Issues

Dramatic story-issues revolve around issues of human need. The need to be loved. To have control of one's fate. To feel a sense of purpose. To be able to overcome obstacles. To be able to grow and heal from life's wounds. To understand and make sense of the events of life.

It is important that you are able to *name*, in your own words, the dramatic issue at the heart of your story. The opening scenes of your story should clearly suggest it is the beginning of a journey, and that you understand how to create this journey.

If perceiving your story's main dramatic issue is difficult for you, think about the issues in your life that you enjoy seeing acted out as stories. Then put a "name" on those issues. Do they revolve around finding love? Gaining knowledge? Good defeating evil?

If you can't name the issue at the heart of your story, it risks being unclear to your audience. Once you understand that issue, you can go back and edit your opening scenes to a clear dramatic purpose.

If you need to write a story to discover the issue at its heart, that's fine. There is no one path that leads to this understanding.

Movement

The second part of a premise identifies the movement of a story. I believe that the idea of movement in storytelling is a fundamental key to understanding the craft of storytelling. This concept of movement has three interweaving facets.

First, by setting a story in motion toward a destination, a storyteller demonstrates an ability to transport an audience.

To understand the general movement of a story—fear to courage, hate to love, ignorance to understanding—enables a storyteller to better understand what types of characters, events, and environments serve the dramatic purpose of a particular story. A story might express movement toward an illumination of ideas. A journey of feelings. A physical or thoughtful journey toward a new understanding of life.

That is the first meaning I assign to the idea of story movement. It is a demonstration of a storyteller's ability to introduce a story issue and give it a sense of direction and movement toward a goal.

The second meaning of movement revolves around how an audience experiences a story. In a well-told story about a character moving from being fearful to courageous, a story's audience is led to internalize or thoughtfully observe this character's progression. The audience feels *moved* from a state of fear to courage; from one state of perception about the meaning of fear and courage to a new understanding, or moved toward an affirmation of beliefs.

When a story journey is experienced in a potent, vivid way, an audience feels an inner quality of being purposefully moved through different states of feelings, thoughts, and perceptions to states of resolution and fulfillment. Since life does not operate to move people to experience these deeper states of resolution, people perceive quite clearly when a story moves them in an emotional or thoughtful way. Or, conversely, when a story leaves them feeling unmoved. It's why badly constructed stories so quickly put off an audience.

31

The effect of being unmoved is immediate and visceral.

A story is dramatically inert—lacking movement—when no issue of human need is introduced in a way that engages the attention and emotions of an audience. When a storyteller compounds that with a failure to advance toward some state of potent resolution and fulfillment shared by the audience, a story is, as Shakespeare put it, "All sound and fury, signifying nothing."

The third and last issue of story movement I want to define revolves around narrative tension. As a character in a story about courage (or any other expression of movement around an issue of human need) overcomes issues of fear, it is the job of the storyteller to transfer the tension from the story's characters to its audience. Once a story's audience has fully internalized a need for a story's characters, events or ideas to have resolution and fulfillment, that audience desires to experience a story's resolution. That offers members of a story's audience a relief from their own narrative tension around unresolved feelings and beliefs. This is a powerful experience.

Once the members of an audience are fully enmeshed in a story's dramatic movement, the members of that audience desire, need, to experience a story's resolution and fulfillment for the relief it offers.

This is why understanding the different facets of movement are so vital for struggling, inexperienced storytellers. Such writers are often taught to focus on concepts like developing a particular kind of plot, introducing certain types of characters, or learning to use descriptive language. None of that, alone, generates narrative tension. Without narrative tension, words are just lifeless smudges of ink on a page, boring images on a film screen, or tedious characters on a stage.

To understand the movement of a story, then, is to see into the heart of a story, and what kind of journey it promises its audience, and why an audience desires a particular story journey. Understanding story movement—or its lack on any of these three levels—can lead to an understanding of why audiences turn away so quickly from stories that fail to generate this internal quality of narrative tension that the storyteller both creates and relieves.

To sum up this idea of movement as it relates to a story's promise and its premise...

A story's promise speaks directly to the issue of human need that a story explores. It offers a reason for an audience to enter into a story's world.

A story premise speaks to the mechanics of how that issue of human need will be introduced, the path it takes toward resolution and fulfillment, and what will make concrete a story's fulfillment of its premise for both its characters and audience.

That a story must operate to transport characters toward a heightened state of resolution and fulfillment, while at the same time resolving issues and story concepts in a way that emotionally or thoughtfully moves an audience to an intense experience of dramatic relief, makes the concept of movement in storytelling both simple and difficult to understand. Gaining that understanding is a path toward learning to be a storyteller.

I know my conception of story movement is difficult to explain and to understand. Some of my students have needed years to fully understand the concept. I also know from working with writers that some facet of weak movement is the benchmark of the struggling storyteller's efforts. But, once a storyteller understands fully this concept of story movement, every well-told story and every badly told story offers a lesson because the "why" of the story's strengths and weaknesses is fully apparent.

To complete my definition of premise, I'll now discuss the third aspect of a premise—fulfillment.

Fulfillment

A story's fulfillment is what a story's characters gain or achieve from the resolution of a story's promise...

and...

...the heightened feelings, thoughts, perceptions, and affirmations of beliefs a story's resolution offers a story's audience.

I offer this dual definition of fulfillment because a storyteller both writes *toward* a physical, emotional or thoughtful destination (a character finding their way home and what that means, for example), and *about* that destination with an understanding of the feelings, thoughts, and perceptions that reaching this place generates for an audience. To not write with this dual understanding is to risk having an ending that resolves the action of a story in a way that satisfies the storyteller, but leaves the storyteller's audience unmoved, unfulfilled, or unsatisfied. No fulfillment, no story magic. It's a bumbling magician who fails to create a good trick.

Because so many events of life leave people feeling unfulfilled, a story that offers a powerful fulfillment can create tremendous inner feeling of relief, a cessation of conflicted and unresolved feelings and ideas. When the hero saves the world, we share that ability and experience. When the underdog rises up to defeat an oppressor, we experience that we can defeat that which oppresses us in life. When the unloved finds true love, we share that experience of love, and we are able to feel we could have the same experience in our own lives. When God saves the world in a story, we can feel we are God's chosen. In those moments, the inner voices that whisper to us that our lives lack meaning, that we will never escape that which oppresses us, or that we don't deserve to be loved, or saved, are silenced.

This makes a good story something that people hunger for. Good stories meet needs buried deep in the human mind and heart. Or, for some people good stories offer salve for emotional wounds that are raw and aching and in need of constant story medication.

To understand fulfillment, consider what your favorite stories led you to feel or think. What feelings about life did you have renewed, affirmed, enlivened? What epiphanies about life did you experience? That is each story's fulfillment. That is what you create for an audience as a storyteller.

What I often find in stories that lack a strong quality of fulfillment is that storytellers are overlaying personal feelings about story characters and ideas onto a story's events. They do this without realizing their writing isn't generating a satisfying fulfillment for an audience. That is why I teach premise. To help storytellers see into the heart of a story and to understand both why it affects them, and how a story can be told in a way that it affects—transports—an audience.

I call writing intended to be storylike that fails to create the effect of fulfillment journaling. This kind of writing is meant for the writer to explore his or her own feelings and experience a relief from their personal narrative tension around life issues through the actions of their characters. Such writers are the audience for their stories. These kind of stories can work, but often I see struggling storytellers creating novels around characters who are 'stuck' because that's the basic life situation/feeling for the author. These novels often end with the main character finally free to act, which would be the beginning of a story. But, at that point the authors have found relief of their own feelings, so they have no need to continue, and they often are bewildered why others find their journals/accounts dramatically unsatisfying. It's an evening spent looking at slides of someone else's vacation gettaway.

A premise can help writers avoid this situation by understanding the fulfillment a story offers an audience.

To visualize a premise, think of it as a house foundation. Just like a foundation supports a well-constructed house, a story premise supports a well-constructed story. Like a house foundation, it is not meant to be artistic or original so much as clear and direct in setting out a story's main dramatic issue, and what action dramatically advances a story toward its fulfillment.

To visualize this, consider a community of expensive homes. Every home would likely be different, unique, expressive. Now think of that community burned to the ground. After the fire, when all that's left are bare foundations, all the foundations have a similar quality. They all tend to look alike.

A premise is like that. It's not meant to be different, artistic, or unique. It's meant to set a foundation that supports the more visible aspects of a story, its characters and events, just as a house's foundation supports the more visible aspects of a house, its walls, roof, windows, etc. Just like a house foundation, a story's foundation is not meant to be visible to an audience. It's meant to serve the purpose of the storyteller, the builder of the story.

Different storytellers could start with the premise of *Romeo and Juliet* and write entirely different stories. Each storyteller would bring a different writing style, word choices, characters, plot events, ideas, and concepts to create the same premise.

Lajos Egri in *The Art of Dramatic Writing* [13] explores the concept of premise. His premise for *Romeo and Juliet* is "Great love defies even death." (The Art of Dramatic Writing, Page 15.)

The dramatic issue in this story is love. Because readers desire to experience love in a fulfilling way, love as a dramatic issue is at the heart of many stories. It is an issue many people will choose to become emotionally invested in.

The dramatic movement of *Romeo and Juliet* is about love overcoming obstacles that escalate to include death. By defying even death, the story fulfills its premise. It is a story about great love. The word "defying" describes the movement of the story. The characters must defy everything that stands in the way of their love. Shakespeare's job was to keep making those obstacles larger and larger, rising to include death, normally an obstacle that cannot be overcome.

Note, also, that to defy something suggests drama. What will this defiance lead to, gain, lose, cost? From the opening scenes of a story, it should be clear the storyteller understands how to set a story into motion through the introduction of a dramatic situation.

Because every premise expresses an active quality of a story's movement, it can serve as a guide to what constitutes the dramatic beginning of a story. A story about identity might begin with a character being stripped of her identity. Such a character must act to regain that which she has lost. Knowing what a story is about, a storyteller can embed the core dramatic issue of a story in action, dialogue, events, and descriptions of an environment or character.

To manifest a story's movement toward resolution and fulfillment, a story is populated with characters who feel compelled to act to resolve that issue. *Rocky*, for example, is about someone who feels compelled to prove he's somebody by overcoming insurmountable odds.

In *Romeo and Juliet*, the love the title characters feel for each other is threatened by characters who love to hate. The result is conflict between characters who must love and characters designed to block the expression of that love. The unwillingness of both sets of characters to be blocked advances the story dramatically.

Characters who simply have goals opposed by others do not create the effect of a story, however. It is because characters act to advance a dramatic issue toward the resolution and fulfillment of a story's promise that their actions transport an audience in a thoughtfully or emotionally satisfying way.

A subtle point must be made. *Romeo and Juliet* is a story about great—if tragic—love. Its plot operates to make the story's fulfillment dramatic and deeply felt. Its characters create for the audience this experience of great love. But, a storyteller can think about the deeper story issue here, this concept of great love and how it affects an audience, without talking about specific characters or plot events. This is sometimes necessary to help create characters who are fully enmeshed and committed to gaining a goal that arises from a story's promise.

Don't worry, then, if your premise seems too simple. It's meant to help you understand your story in a clear, direct way. Once you understand how to create a dynamic story premise, it will help you with every other element of storytelling, such as what kinds of characters might populate your story, how to create plot events that serve to make your story's movement dramatic, and which characters' actions and story events best manifest your story's fulfillment.

Or, you might write your story first, then explore it to see the premise that lies at its heart. Then, use that new understanding of your story to guide rewrites.

The ability to create a premise offers writers an opportunity to understand the foundation of a story *before* they begin to write it. Such an understanding can help writers avoid multiple rewrites in an attempt to "find" their story.

Whatever form for creating a premise works for you—one sentence, three, a full page of notes, or creating an entire novel, screenplay, or play to discover a premise—do what works best for you. A premise is a tool meant to help you. If you can write well-told stories without creating or understanding how to create a premise, good for you. If creating a premise leaves you uninterested in creating a story now that you know where it's going, then don't create a premise. But, if you struggle to tell stories—if your stories lack a strong beginning, middle and end, dynamic characters, a plot that creates rising tension, endings that are fulfilling, or a lack of narrative tension—I suggest you keep on trying to learn and understand how to create and use a story premise.

If you can learn to use a premise to understand how to both promise an engaging story journey to an audience, and how to fulfill that promise, your writing will improve.

In the following chapter, I offer techniques for creating a story premise.

Chapter Questions

What dramatic issue most appeals to you in stories?

How do the stories you enjoy most move their core dramatic issue toward resolution?

Are you giving your story characters the freedom to act out their own story issues, or using them to act out your own issues in life?

Can you create premises for some of your favorite stories?

Techniques of Creating a Story Premise

To create a premise, start by writing three sentences. The first should lay out the dramatic issue that arises from your story's promise. The second, your story's movement toward the resolution of your story's promise. The third, your story's fulfillment of its promise.

To begin, write a sentence that starts:

My story is about...

Using the movie *Rocky* as an example, the dramatic issue at the heart of the premise is about self-respect. A simple way to state that:

Rocky is a story about gaining self-respect.

Gaining self-respect, a sense of mattering, is the dramatic issue at the heart of many stories.

When you write your sentence, write about the dramatic issue or idea at the heart of your story, not character goals or plot devices. Love, hate, redemption, rebirth, the desire for revenge, courage: these are the kinds of dramatic issues and ideas found at the heart of stories.

Second, write a sentence that begins:

The movement of my story toward the resolution of its promise can be described as...

Does your story's advance center around overcoming, defeating, understanding, or avenging something? Is the action of your story leading to something, such as rebirth, or redemption, or renewal? A sentence that describes the movement of *Rocky* could read:

Rocky is a story about someone discovering within himself the courage to overcome insurmountable obstacles.

Again, be clear that you're writing about the movement of your story toward its dramatic destination, not just describing the actions of your main character to attain a personal goal. You must make this distinction because the action of every character in your story should contribute to your story's overall movement toward its resolution and fulfillment.

Third, write a sentence that begins:

The fulfillment of my story is…

The fulfillment of *Rocky* is that Rocky's courage to overcome the odds proves he is somebody to himself and the world. He achieves a self-respect he lacked. Because there's a need in our world to believe that if we just had enough courage we could prove to the world that we are somebody, this story drew audiences to experience its powerful fulfillment. Through Rocky's character, others experienced how courage and belief in oneself could be transforming.

The premise of *Rocky* can be reduced to one sentence:

The courage to persevere in the face of overwhelming obstacles leads to self-respect.

Now, I want you to look over your three sentences and reduce them to a single sentence. Begin by writing:

The premise of my story is…

Was it a struggle for you to think of your story in terms of a single sentence? If it was, look over what you've written. Return to my analogy of a premise as a house's foundation. Are you trying to actually build a house when you write your premise? A premise is a simple, solid statement, in the same way that a house foundation is a solid, simple structure. When I work with people struggling with writing a premise, it is usually because they're trying to use a premise to tell a story—the characters went here and did this, this is the plot, etc.

The premise of *Romeo and Juliet* would never begin:

Romeo is a young man who falls in love with Juliet, and to be with her, he must…

Again, that leads writers to mistake character goals for what's at the heart of their stories.

39

Examples of other faulty premises include:

History creates change.

This premise is too general. It is not specific about what kinds of events create history. It doesn't set out how this history acts on some group of people in a way that a story would offer resolution or fulfillment of particular issues.

The premise could be recast as:

War leads to senseless destruction.

This premise is still general, but it is more specific about what war can lead to. The active verb, "leads to," suggests this story is moving toward a destination. The specific fulfillment identified by the premise, "destruction," describes the outcome of the story. This is a premise one could use to answer the question: What kind of characters and events bring this story to life?

What's at stake in this story is whether the destruction of war can be avoided. For this particular story premise, the answer would be no. In this story, the destruction of war would ruin both victor and defeated. That defeat might be material, moral, or physical; that is a choice of the storyteller.

A more uplifting premise about war could be:

The destruction of war leads to rebirth.

While this story would have the same background as the premise above, it would move toward a different fulfillment. The fulfillment of this story might be that out of the aftermath of war and its destruction, life begins anew. This could be shown through a character's renewal, or the renewal of a country.

Another false premise is:

Love is its own reward.

This premise is not specific. What kind of love does this story talk about? What kind of reward? Keep in mind that a moral is not a premise. While a moral might give insight into some state of human need or state of affairs, it is not a premise because it does not suggest a state of dramatic advance toward a specific destination.

To make the above a premise, it could be rewritten as: Going through the pain of young love leads to growth. Such a premise would be a natural in a coming-of-age novel. Now the premise refers to a specific kind of dramatic issue with a specific movement and a clear fulfillment. In a possible story based on this premise, two teens might meet, have a rocky relationship, break up, and date others. But, through those events, they come to a deeper, richer understanding of love. Because most people have their own painful memories or experiences of young love, a story that offers a dramatic, deeply felt, positive outcome to such a dramatic issue is pleasurable.

One more false premise:

Hate destroys itself.

This has a focus on a dramatic issue and movement, but it needs to be more specific about its fulfillment. Recast it as: Hate destroys those who wield it as a weapon.

See how that premise suggests the characters who would populate that particular story world? How its movement suggests the way in which the story progresses? And its fulfillment?

If you're still having trouble writing a premise, consider your main character and answer the following questions. What goal motivates your main character? Rocky, for example, desires to prove that he is somebody.

What verb would you use to describe your main character's actions—what they must do—to attain what he or she seeks? In *The Hunt for Red October*, Ramius battles the communist system of oppression that denies him his freedom.

Lastly, what makes concrete the fulfillment of your character attaining some goal? Rocky's fulfillment is that he feels he is somebody and that the rest of the world knows it.

Ramius gains his freedom. Scrooge is renewed. Dorothy learns valuable lessons about herself and what's important in life.

Once you understand how to create a dynamic story premise, it will help you understand the kinds of characters who populate your story's world; how to create plots that serve to make your story's movement dramatic; how to understand what character actions and story events best manifest your story's fulfillment; or how to explore your story to find the premise that lies at its heart and use that to guide rewrites.

A well-designed premise is a cornerstone of a story foundation.

Chapter Questions

How does your premise set out your story's promise in an active voice?
How does the goal that your main character seeks to resolve move your story toward its fulfillment?
How does your premise describe your story's fulfillment?

Characters, Story, and Premise

Because a story's characters promise to take the story's audience on a rewarding journey, dynamic, active characters are an important—often vital—element of a story.

Because story characters resolve issues of human need they engage the attention of an audience. When introducing a story's characters, then, writers need to suggest in some way that their characters are "ripe." For example, if love is the main issue in a story's premise, the storyteller can give a character an issue of love to resolve in a story's opening scenes. Romeo and Juliet are designed to be strong-willed characters in love with the idea of love. They are separated by characters who love to hate. But Romeo and Juliet love even unto death, refusing to let it be an obstacle to their love. By their actions, they bring this story about love to life in a way readers have enjoyed for centuries. Because their actions arise from and act out the story's premise, they manifest the story's movement to fulfillment.

Introducing characters with story issues that resonate with a particular audience also draws an audience into a story. For example, a story aimed at teenage boys might call for a protagonist of interest to that audience. A story aimed at an audience of middle-aged women would have a different protagonist. This is not to make a value judgment about either story; rather, it is to say that the storyteller must design his characters for the particular fulfillment he wants to create for the intended audience.

To give your audience a reason to identify with your characters, have your characters react with strong feelings and actions to a story's events. In a story about redemption, characters could confront feelings about redemption. How they react both names the story and gives voice to the character's feelings. By resolving a character's coflict around the feelings aroused by the events of a story, a story has meaning to those in the audience with similar feelings and issues.

No matter how compelling a story's dramatic issue, a story needs characters clearly compelled to resolve its issues. One way to introduce such characters is in situations where they are actively attempting to achieve goals. And if their goals arise from a particular story's premise, their actions will advance the story itself.

Indiana Jones, in *Raiders of the Lost Ark*[14], is introduced as an adventurous character who must deal with immediate and pressing issues of trust and morality. In *L.A. Confidential*[15], three men are stripped of their identities and have to struggle to regain a sense of who they are. In The *Sixth Sense*[16], a psychologist who misdiagnosed a boy, leading to fatal consequences, gets a second chance to help another boy with similar problems.

You can also introduce characters in odd, unusual, or active environments. James Bond films often open with dramatic action scenes meant to be thrilling and unique, but that also *names* a story issue. *Speed*[17] took an old idea and made it fresh by having the action revolve around a bus that would blow up if it slowed to less than fifty miles per hour. *The Limey*[18], a wonderful film directed by Steven Soderberg, opens on a black screen with a man's voice urgently asking, "Tell me, tell me about Jenny."

If there's nothing interesting about the environment you're using to introduce a character, why did you choose it? Can you make a better choice? Are you describing your environment in a way that clearly impacts your audience? Think of your story environment as a character in your story, rising up to act, to block, to help, to frustrate your main character.

If characters have nothing to do in a scene, edit them out, create a purpose for them, or introduce them later when they do have something to do. A storyteller who begins a story in a static voice with static characters risks an audience turning away. Describing a static character in detail creates details that ring false to an audience.

By carefully choosing how and when to introduce characters in active situations, and describing those situations with details that evoke the action of a scene, a storyteller greatly expands the appeal of a story and its characters to an audience.

Active characters by their very introduction promise something to an audience.

Some writers struggle to create dynamic characters because they project their feelings onto their characters. For example, I worked with one writer who created a main character who was in a 'happy' marriage, but nothing the character did or said suggested he was happy about being married; to the contrary, his complete lack of feeling for his wife suggested otherwise. In this case, the writer projected his own feelings about his marriage onto his character. When all the characters in a story are a projection of the storyteller, the risk is that all the characters have one voice, the storyteller's, and all have one unresolved dramatic truth, the author's. In extreme cases of this, characters come across as soulless, lifeless automatons in the service of their creators.

To create characters who have feelings separate from your own, ask yourself if your characters have their own responses to what they encounter in a story. Do some of your characters love foods you hate, movies you avoid, body types you find distasteful? Create characters who have their own lives, needs, desires, who don't respond to events the way you would. Such characters generate their own subtext to the meaning of events, to a story's environment, to how they view their lives.

Creating and understanding a premise for a story and a story's character is one method to ensure that a character goes into motion to resolve and fulfill clearly defined issues.

Chapter Questions

Who are some of your favorite story characters? Why? What issues did they resolve?

How are some of your characters similar to your favorite story characters?

What are your favorite story characters able to accomplish that you struggle with in life?

When 9/11 happened, did you imagine yourself being a story character involved in stopping the attack? A rescuer?

Did being such a character help you deal with your feelings?

Are you allowing your story characters to be larger than life, to resolve issues that you struggle with, to accomplish goals that are beyond you, or different than your goals?

What *Is* a Plot?

Understanding what a plot is creates a foundation for the ability to create one. Unfortunately, most writers are consumed with the idea of creating the effect of what a plot does without first understanding what a plot is.

What a plot does: It raises dramatic questions that a reader or viewer will want to get answers for.

What a plot is: It is the process of generating questions and drama around the advance toward a story's resolution and the fulfillment of a story's promise.

What a plot is: By blocking a character from gaining what he or she seeks, a plot increases the narrative tension a character experiences; and, by making that tension accessible, transferred to a story's audience.

A good plot both heightens a story's narrative tension in a story's audience and relieves that tension in a powerful way.

In any story, as characters act to achieve goals and resolve their dramatic truths, their actions should advance the story toward its resolution and fulfillment. Because other characters are driven to shape a story to their own design and dramatic truths, these opposing characters are naturally in conflict. As different characters act and block each other, they generate new obstacles to each other's progress. This escalates the drama around a story's outcome.

The purpose of a story's plot is to make a story's progression toward resolution and fulfillment dramatic. But it's only when a story's events are in motion toward a common destination that there is any movement to block. Further, without any dramatic tension around a story's movement, a story appears to be a collection of incidents. Such incidents may be dramatic in their own right, but collectively they fail to engage the interest of an audience. They fail because they lack a discernible dramatic purpose.

The key here is to understand that to describe a story about love is not to describe its plot. A story is about an issue of human need; a plot is a way of heightening the tension over that issue being acted out to resolution.

Romeo and Juliet is an example of a well-crafted plot that heightens the dramatic effect of a simple story. By loving each other in spite of the mutual hatred of their families, Romeo and Juliet set the story in motion. But it is the story's plot that makes the story's movement dramatic. By generating obstacles that block the young lovers from being together, the storyteller creates a plot that makes the lover's plight more dramatic. Even knowing the story's outcome, the action of its plot—moment by moment—generates for the story's audience a dramatic experience of an undeniable love.

To illustrate how a plot grows from a story's premise, consider the novel *The Hunt for Red October.* On the surface it appears to be a plot-driven thriller about a commander of a Russian nuclear submarine attempting to flee to America and freedom. The core story issue here revolves around a battle between freedom and authoritarianism. The issue of human need in this story is a man's desire to be free of oppression. This is laid out in the story's premise: The courage to battle oppression leads to freedom.

Because readers desire to experience the values of freedom winning over oppression, they readily internalize this story's movement. Because the story in its every action proved its premise, it rewarded its readers. Its highly praised plot succeeded because it made the conflict of the freedom battling oppression clear, dramatic, and accessible.

Tom Clancy succeeded in creating a great plot because he understood how to create a plot that manifested the movement of his story toward a specific resolution and fulfillment. Every character, situation, and action grew out of his story's promise and existed in the world it created. To the extent readers feel emotionally or thoughtfully enmeshed in whether or not Ramius gains his freedom, they must find out how the story ends. That ending offers readers a share of Ramius's victory, and relief from the narrative tension over whether he would gain that victory or not.

When someone is compelled to finish your story to see how it turns out, your plot has fulfilled its purpose.

The writer who doesn't see the connection between a story, its characters, and plot risks introducing characters or plot devices that have no real bearing on a story's course or ultimate destination. Setting up a situation common to action films, "Who's going to get out of here alive," is plot-like. Lacking a deeper story issue, however, such films struggle to engage a wide audience. Simply tacking on a story issue to an action plot is not the answer, either. A strong story issue must be woven through all the elements of a story if it is to powerfully affect an audience.

In *The Winslow Boy*[19], a play by Terence Rattigan adapted for film by David Mamet, the story's plot revolves around whether or not a young boy wrongly accused of a crime can find justice. The deeper truth of the story is the price this justice costs, and whether the story's characters are willing to pay it. As the price of truth escalates, the story's plot strikes at the story's characters, compelling them to reveal the truth of their feelings about what price they will pay for justice. Again and again, the plot strikes at these characters, compelling deeper and deeper revelations. A story's plot must operate to propel characters to experience these potent revelations of truth. Without such plot-fueled revelations, the description of the actions of characters remain cold and lifeless.

To create a great plot, start with your premise. Understand how what's at stake over your story's outcome raises questions to which your audience is led to desire answers. Understand that your plot should make the journey to get those answers potent and dramatic.

When your audience is fully invested in the outcome of your story, that's when you'll be told, "Wow! Loved your plot!"

Chapter Questions

How does your plot escalate the drama around your story's course and outcome?

How do the events of your plot name your story?

How does your plot operate to give your characters a clear dramatic purpose?

How does your plot make your story's fulfillment dramatic?

Creating a Dramatic Plot

What is the main dramatic issue of your story? Hate? Desire? Courage? Rebirth? Redemption? Revenge? When George Lucas was asked what *Star Wars*[20] was about, he had a one word answer: Redemption.

Perceiving your story's central dramatic issue should help you identify what's at stake in your story. If you've identified the dramatic issue of your story, finish this sentence:

> *The central issue at stake over the outcome of my story is…*

You should be able to answer this question without mentioning your characters. It is the job of your characters to manifest the answer, but the answer is separate from them. Once you're able to verbalize your story's core dramatic issue, you must perceive how your plot operates to make its movement toward resolution dramatic.

To do that, finish the following sentence:

> *My plot serves to escalate the drama over my story's outcome by placing the following obstacles before my character(s)…*

Be clear that the actions of your characters advance your story toward its outcome. To win his freedom, Ramius must escape to America in the *Red October* by outwitting the combined forces of the Soviet and American navies and governments. Ramius manifests the premise of the story, that the values of freedom can defeat oppression. His dramatic truth is that he will not be denied his freedom.

One of the issues that can make a plot seem so compelling is that it raises a dramatic story question. In *The Hunt for Red October* that question is:

> *Will Ramius make it to America and gain his freedom?*

To get the answer, one has to read—is compelled to read—to the end of the story.

For your story, complete the following:

Readers will care about the outcome of my story because they care about the outcome of the following character's dramatic truth...

This is where the ability to create characters who have dramatic truths to resolve comes into play. First, you must have an ability to create characters driven to resolve the issue at your story's heart because of their emotional makeup, beliefs, goals in life, and their determination to gain what they want. Second, you must understand how your plot serves to make their actions compelling and dramatic.

Finish the following:

The plot of my story raises the following story question...

That a story can have a story question and a plot question can mask which is which. Together, they operate to draw an audience through a story. Unfortunately, that is one reason inexperienced writers confuse plot with story. The story question for *The Hunt for Red October* is whether or not Ramius will gain his freedom. The plot question is whether or not he'll manage to escape to America in the *Red October*.

Tom Clancy succeeded in creating a great plot because he understood how to create a plot that manifested the movement of his story toward resolution. His story question revolved around whether Ramius would be able to gain his freedom. His plot question revolved around what actions would gain him his freedom.

To confuse these two issues is to risk creating a series of questions that have no dramatic impact on a story's characters or its audience. In a weak story, there's no underlying sense of why a story's characters or audience should care about the outcome of events, hence no narrative tension. Recognizing the distinction between a story and plot question can help writers avoid that trap.

Some writers succumb to the danger of introducing characters and then creating false plot elements to generate dramatic tension. No matter how dramatic such plot devices appear in isolation, if they do not heighten the effect of a story's advance toward its resolution, they fail to meet the expectations they raise. Therefore, any issues injected into *The Hunt for Red October* not tied to its premise would not serve the story because they would not affect its outcome.

To create a great plot, start with your premise. Understand how what's at stake in your story raises questions for which your audience desires answers. Understand that your plot should make the journey to get those answers potent and dramatic. When you start to write, be clear about the obstacles that block the movement of your story. That force your characters to act with ever greater determination if they would shape your story's outcome.

Chapter Questions

How do the events of your plot operate to block the movement of your story?

How does your plot operate to escalate the drama over the course of your story?

How does your plot operate to escalate the drama over the outcome of your story's promise?

If you look at your life as a story, what is the central issue that you've strived to accomplish in life in spite of obstacles? Are you creating characters who act with the same passion and committment?

What's at Stake in Your Story?

Why do a story's characters persevere to the end of a story? The storyteller provides a clear indication at the outset that something of consequence is at stake that a story's characters feel compelled to resolve.

Why do readers read to the end of a story? Because they have become emotionally or thoughtfully invested in how a story's characters will resolve and fulfill what's at stake.

A writer trying to see clearly what's at stake in a particular story should look to his or her premise and its core dramatic issue. Is it about love? Fear of death? Rebirth? Redemption? What must be overcome or changed by the telling of the story for this issue to be resolved? That's what's at stake.

While characters shape a story's course and outcome, it's only when what's at stake in a story is visible are those in an audience led to feel invested in the outcome of those actions. Writers struggle when they keep what's at stake in a story obscure for dramatic effect or a revelation.

In *Romeo and Juliet*, it's clearly set out that Romeo is in love with the idea of love. It's only then that his obsession focuses on Juliet. Also established very early on are the consequences of what will happen if he openly professes his love for her, and she for him. The story's drama grows from whether or not Romeo and Juliet can find a way to be together. By finding a way to be together, in defiance of every obstacle, they prove the premise of the story. What's at stake is whether their love can defy all obstacles, and, by extension, offer the story's audience an experience of great love.

The pitfall for inexperienced writers? That they confuse what's at stake for individual characters with what's at stake in their stories. Thus, they fail to make what's at stake visible and concrete. Consequently, the actions of their characters do not move their stories toward a dramatic resolution. If the consequences of a character's actions are unclear, a story's drama comes across as weak or confusing. Such stories appear to be of no particular consequence, populated by

51

characters working to achieve goals that have no unity of purpose.

To demonstrate how what's at stake in a story can be made concrete, consider the movie *Die Hard*[21]. The premise for the story is:

Courage in the face of adversity leads to renewal.

On the surface, this is a story about a lone New York detective, John McClane, trapped in a building taken over by terrorists. What's visible on the screen is the fighting among McClane, the L.A. police, the FBI, and the terrorists. But what's really at stake is whether McClane can get back together with his wife. By reuniting with her, he proves the story's premise, that having the courage to overcome adversity leads to the renewal of their love.

All the action of *Die Hard* serves as obstacles to McClane shaping the story's outcome in a way desirable to him. The story's fiery, explosive spectacle makes visible the obstacles he must overcome. What's at stake in *Die Hard* draws in viewers to emotionally invest in the story's outcome. By proving its premise, the story lets its audience experience the story's fulfillment when McClane and his wife reunite.

A story like *Die Hard* is more than the sum of its visible action: a lone cop battling terrorists. It's a story that raises an emotional issue that viewers are led to feel invested in. Thus, the film promises a story-like experience of the power of renewal, and fulfills that promise. Its fiery explosions and spectacle are built on a strong foundation. Spectacle without that foundation generally doesn't attract a wide audience, for example, Die Hard III.

In *Honey, I Shrunk the Kids*[22], several children are miniaturized by a scientist-father's invention. The action of the story revolves around how, and if, the children can survive a trek across a back yard to be enlarged again. The story itself is concerned with whether or not the children and their families can overcome this catastrophe and rebond in a loving way.

The story's premise is:

Overcoming a shared catastrophe leads to renewal.

What's at stake is whether these families can overcome this story's catastrophe. The catastrophe of the story sets the stage for this story. The plot of the story revolves around how, and if, this re-bonding will happen, or what might prevent it from happening. The action of the story's plot—the difficulties the children and their parents face—escalates the drama over how what's at stake will be resolved. The consequence of these families not overcoming this catastrophe is death. Because this story has a happy ending, these children and families prove the story's premise, and what's at stake is fulfilled in an uplifting way because the families are renewed.

If what's at stake over a story's promise reaching fulfillment is something an audience wants and needs to believe, the story is emotionally engaging.

In *Batman Forever*[23], what's at stake is that Bruce Wayne (Batman) finds a way to integrate the two sides of his personality. This gives direction to what kind of characters populate the story. The Riddler and Two-Face make visible his inner conflict. Robin as well as Bruce Wayne's therapist also force him to confront his need to integrate his personality.

The action of the story builds to a climax when The Riddler and Two Face confront Batman with making a choice to save either Robin, his new companion, or Kidman, Bruce Wayne's potential lover. The story's action here makes visible what's at stake. Can Wayne-Batman integrate as one personality in time to save his friends? Because Wayne-Batman succeeds in integrating his personality, he is able to save both Robin and Kidman.

In *The Wizard of Oz,* what's at stake for Dorothy is finding that she has a place where she really matters, her home. In *Lethal Weapon*[24], what's at stake for detective Martin Riggs is resolving his grief over his wife's death. The end of the film shows him at her graveside, finally able to let go of his grief and live again.

Within the main question of what's at stake in a story might be dozens of individual issues and conflicts that are raised and resolved as a story progresses. The resolution of these events advances the story toward its fulfillment. If this is not true, they should be eliminated. Just as characters can have something at stake, a scene can also present something at stake. In *Batman Forever,* Bruce Wayne goes to a party where Enigma demonstrates a device. If Bruce Wayne enters it, he reveals his identity as Batman. Just as Bruce Wayne enters the device, Two Face crashes the party. In this scene, several things are at stake for several of the characters: for Two Face, it is finding and killing Batman; for Enigma, it is unmasking Bruce Wayne; for Wayne-Batman, it is keeping his identity masked; for Robin, it is his desire to confront Two Face; and for the therapist accompanying Bruce Wayne, it is resolving her feelings for both Bruce Wayne and Batman.

All of these issues play out in the scene. All push the story forward to resolve what's ultimately at stake: Wayne-Batman integrating his dual nature. In any story, individual scenes have a specific focus and purpose, with a discernible outcome that acts to shape a story's course and outcome. In totality, the scenes of a story advance it toward its fulfillment across a range of levels, plot, story, promise, and character goals. Understanding what's at stake in your story and how to make it visible offers you another tool to ensure your story resonates with an audience. How can you do this?

Put your characters into a situation where they react with strong feelings. Feelings that compel them to take action.

As your plot heightens the impact of what's at stake for you characters, the reactions of your characters should change. Revelations about what drives your characters should become deeper. Actions compelled by these revelations are more forceful, more desperate. Feelings should become deeper and more potent.

Many stories have a character whom the main character can talk to about feelings or plans that shape events. Find a way to let your audience know your characters clearly feel something is at stake in the course and outcome of the story world you've created.

Have your characters act out their feelings when they've resolved what's at stake in your story.

Ask yourself, how do you make visible what's at stake in your story in your opening scenes? How do you make visible how your characters feel about what's at stake in your story?

When you can clearly communicate that something is at stake in the world of your story in your opening scenes, you let your audience know you understand how to tell a dramatic story.

Creating characters who act to resolve what's at stake over dramatic issues arising from a story's promise is a sure path to writing dynamic stories.

Chapter Questions

What's at stake in your story?
What's at stake for the main character in your story?
What's at stake for the character who opposes your main character?
How do you resolve what's at stake in your story?
What events make it clear what's at stake for your main character?
What events make it clear what's at stake for the character who opposes your main character?

What *Is* Conflict?

On the surface, conflict in a story appears to be characters in opposition, events in collision, ideas in a battle for supremacy. Just as with trying to understand a plot based on what it appears to be rather than what it is, trying to understand what conflict is by describing what it looks like leads to a faulty understanding of what conflict in a story is.

Conflict in a story is a manifestation of a story's movement. When a storyteller creates movement toward resolving some compelling idea, issue, character goal, or event, and then blocks that movement, the result is conflict. By creating conflict around an issue that resonates with both a story's characters and its audience, the storyteller heightens the dramatic effect of a story's conflict.

The catch is, if characters aren't collectively moving toward something—a personal goal, an outcome for events—they cannot block each other or otherwise have a discernible reason to come into contact. Such characters are simply in the service of a plot, moved around by the storyteller, but not acting on their own dramatic truths.

Just as character details that serve no discernible dramatic purpose weaken a story, conflict that serves no purpose is ultimately dramatically inert. Random, purposeless conflict fails to fuel the advance of a story toward resolution and fulfillment. Two parked cars don't suggest the possibility of an imminent collision between them.

When a character is designed to feel compelled to overcome the obstacles that block him or her, the result is escalating conflict. Story elements that create that blocking effect serve to escalate the drama over whether and how a story will advance. Stories that lack events that block their advance lack conflict. Thus, the actions of characters that do not operate around advancing or blocking a story's movement fail to create a discernible quality of story-like conflict (conflict that heightens the dramatic effect of a story) for an audience.

Conflict only rings "true" when it serves a dramatic purpose. Otherwise, it's a flame that doesn't burn, an explosion with no force, heated dialogue spoken with no volume.

The conflict around a story's advance is not necessarily physical. It can involve ideas or feelings in conflict, or it can revolve around a struggle for understanding or even around a set of beliefs being tested or explored. Conflict can also be generated by focusing on what blocks a story's characters from gaining the insights that enable them to overcome the obstacles that block their path.

The issue here is that the storyteller comprehend the movement of a story toward resolution and fulfillment and how and why it is carried out by a story's characters and events. In that sense, a story's conflict and movement are a separate if interwoven issue from the goals and conflict that drive particular characters. It is because a story's characters and their goals do entwine with what's at stake in the story that their actions generate a quality of story-like conflict with a discernible purpose. Because the actions of Romeo and Juliet prove their love for each other in spite of any obstacles, the story's conflict highlights the fulfillment of its premise in a dramatic way.

Only when characters are willing to engage in conflict do their actions communicate that what's at stake in the story has value to them. Therefore, conflict is the pulse, the life force, of a healthy story. A story that lacks that pulse is dead because no one cares enough about its promise or its outcome to act.

Conflict in a story, then, is not simply two characters with opposing goals. A manuscript filled with such characters often fails to create the effect of story-like conflict. Only when the conflict at the heart of a story serves a dramatic purpose (generating resolution and fulfillment for an audience, and a heightened release of narrative tenson) does it create the effect of a story.

To understand the conflict at the heart of your story, you must understand what fuels the advance of your story and what blocks that advance. Then, you should populate your story with characters who will not be blocked. Who will not be denied. Who will not be resisted. Who will not be put down as they try and shape the outcome of your story's promise.

Characters who have opposing dramatic truths are naturally in conflict. For example, a character who wants to be rooted in a particular time or place will be in conflict with a character who insists they move. A character determined to avoid being in love will be in conflict with a character who demands love. A character who wants freedom will be in conflict with someone who seeks to oppress him or her.

In the Harry Potter novels, the narrative tension that revolves around Harry being a magician and having a place to fit into that world, and the Dursley's hatred of magic and their desire to block Harry from that world, radiates from the chronicles of Harry's adventures. Harry Potter novels, no matter that they are aimed at a young audience, are chronicles of relentless narrative tension and powerful conflict.

If you avoid conflict in life, be aware of whether you're creating story characters who are extensions of you, who avoid conflict as well. In such stories, significant conflict often happens off stage, where it risks being unfelt and seemingly unimportant to an audience.

In life, we avoid conflict and the tension it unleashes. In stories, characters often initiate conflict at every turn. That conflict heightens both a story's narrative tension and the power of the release that tension offers. If you want a large audience, learn how to put your characters into conflict that involves, consumes and releases your audience.

If you give your characters the freedom and will to engage in deeply felt conflict, you give your audience a powerful gift.

Chapter Questions

Why are your characters willing to engage in conflict to shape the outcome of your story?

What events in your story block your characters from achieving their goals?

What conflicts do you avoid in life, and how does that impact the kind of conflict you enjoy experiencing in stories?

What kinds of conflict do you enjoy in life? Find arousing? Stimulating?

Describe the conflict around your characters shaping the outcome of your story's promise.

Escalating Your Story's Conflict

Because characters feel the pull of what's at stake in a story and over resolving their dramatic truths, they act to shape a story's outcome. As the storyteller deliberately increases the obstacles characters must overcome, the characters must act with greater determination. The result is dramatic action in the form of escalating conflict.

To explore the relationship between character goals, premise, and conflict, consider *Romeo and Juliet* once more. The conflict arises from the fact that Romeo and Juliet are *deliberately* separated by those who hate. Because Romeo and Juliet believe in love but belong to families who are in love with hate, there can be no compromise. These characters have opposing dramatic truths.

If Romeo and Juliet can find a way to be together, love is able to defy all the obstacles that hate puts in its path. Conversely, if Romeo and Juliet cannot find a way to fulfill their love, the story would prove that hate is stronger than love. A story's audience generally desires a fulfilling outcome of the story—that love overcomes hate—even if it means the death of Romeo and Juliet. Their deaths in the cause of love heighten the story's dramatic impact exactly because they *are* willing to die to prove their love.

For Romeo and Juliet, what's at stake is not so much the love between them, as the idea of proving the power of their love to themselves. To prove the power of their love, Romeo and Juliet must find a way to be together, no matter the cost. Their conflict is internal as well as external. They are in conflict around living up to their own perceptions of what love should be.

By introducing Romeo and Juliet during a family feud is what is meant by in medias res, i.e. in the middle of things. From the story's opening moments, Shakespeare generates a sense of conflict around the outcome of

Romeo's actions. That Romeo is in conflict in his world is not something that must be established so much as managed.

To intensify and heighten the story's conflict, the Capulets and Montagues are bound together not just by hatred but by physical proximity. And any action on one character's part compels a reaction by another character. The reaction always serves to escalate the story's conflict by creating further obstacles that Romeo and Juliet must overcome.

A story with unripe characters has characters who stand inert and unmoving, no matter how much the storyteller dashes around flinging adjectives and adverbs. This kind of effort at description routinely fails to create the effect of real conflict. Unripe characters are dramatically inert because their actions do not advance the story. Their superficially conflict-fueled actions offer an audience no reason to internalize their goals because they do not revolve around a discernible dramatic purpose.

Because a character's actions tie into a story's premise, blocking the movement of characters causes an escalating level of conflict. This escalation makes a story's drama visible and concrete. That is the purpose of a plot. The escalation in dramatic tension it generates for a story's resolution creates a more deeply felt state of fulfillment for its audience.

As characters act with greater determination, they reveal the feelings and needs that drive them. Because an audience can more easily invest in emotionally accessible characters, conflict-driven characters are desirable to an audience. Through identifying with characters presented in deeply felt states of emotion, a story's audience also shares their heightened state of feelings. A story that lacks conflict often fails to set up those states of charged emotions or intense thoughts and sensory experiences and risks denying a story's audience a prime reason for entering a story's world.

Storytellers *design* the environments their characters operate to block a characters ability to advance toward a goal. Storytellers deliberately design a story's environment with as much purpose as they describe other elements of a story— to make more potent and dramatic its effect on a story's audience. Harry Potter, for example, goes to school at Hogwarts, a magical place where inanimate objects often come to life.

Scrooge is taken into an environment—spiritual realms—where he is powerless to avoid confronting his past, present, and future. Dorothy in *The Wizard of Oz* must overcome obstacles in an environment shaped by her private fears. Cinderella struggles to exist in a world where her beauty is a threat and an affront to her step-sisters and mother.

A story fueled by escalating conflict compels characters to achieve goals and break through to a new sense of who they are. This epiphany makes the fulfillment of a story both potent and dramatic. Rocky's courage to fight Apollo Creed and remain on his feet at the end of the fight gives him a new sense of self-respect. Dorothy, by confronting her fears, comes to appreciate who she is, and to appreciate her parents and friends. Harry Potter, by fighting for what he believes, finds a place in life he can fit in, at least until the next sequel.

These characters take audiences on story journeys fraught with dramatic conflict. In turn, that conflict makes each character's journey all the more dramatically fulfilling to an audience.

Chapter Questions

What conflict is inherent in fulfilling your story's promise?

How do you introduce the conflict at the heart of your story?

How does the goal of your main character put him or her into conflict with either the other characters in your story or with himself or herself?

Can you describe the conflict at the heart of your favorite story?

Can you describe the conflict at the heart of your life?

Can you see how your conflicts in life affect what kinds of stories are more emotionally or thoughtfully engaging for you?

The Relationship Between Stories and Ideas

The relationship between a story and the ideas embedded in it is both subtle and profound. My objective here is to help writers perceive the relationship between a story and the ideas that bring it to life. When writers confuse this issue, they come to believe that if they create a story with the required number of ideas, or base a story on ideas that are original or unique, they will create the effect of a dramatic story. That is not true. A storyteller creates the effect of a story by understanding the process of how a story arranges its elements—its ideas, characters, events—to create a discernible, dramatic progression toward resolution and fulfillment.

A thoughtful storyteller can be taught to see that the elements of a story can also represent ideas. Consider *Romeo and Juliet*. Romeo and Juliet convince us that great love can defy even death. Romeo does this by wooing Juliet, gaining her love, and dying to prove his love for her. Juliet, finding Romeo dead, joins him in death, so proving her love for him. The characters in this story take concrete actions that prove the premise of the story, and consequently the story's audience is led to experience the power of great love.

A central issue in this story, however, is also the idea of love. What does it mean to love someone the way Romeo loves Juliet? Is it right that his feelings should lead him to act in a way that brings tragedy to his family? What does Romeo owe his family? His clan? Should his allegiance be to them or to Juliet? What does Juliet owe her clan? Her father?

These are some of the ideas the story explores. By raising and exploring ideas that arise from what's at stake in the story, it becomes clear that these ideas are rooted in—arise from acting out—the story's premise. Because this story's ideas are rooted in and arise from its premise, how they are presented serves to create a quality of discernible advance toward resolution and illumination. Every idea in a story must operate to make a story's advance visible and concrete. Ideas that don't serve that purpose are superfluous and dramatically inert, no matter how they might appear in isolation.

As part of this process of making a distinction between story and idea, consider that the premise of *Romeo and Juliet* can also be seen as an idea, an idea about love that has within it still other ideas. By how these ideas are presented, they become part of the process of the story dramatically offering illumination around the idea of love. Because a story like *Romeo and Juliet* represents ideas as well as characters and events, directors and actors can choose to emphasize a particular idea or ideas in the story. One version of the play could emphasize the idea of whether Romeo should have been more subservient to his clan instead of to his feelings. Another could emphasize Juliet's rebelling against her parent's arrangement of her marriage, thus showing that the issue of a woman having control of her fate is not just a current one. The idea that young people should have some right to choose a mate would be in the service of the story. In a culture where it was unthinkable for a young couple to have any say about whom they marry, the "idea" of *Romeo and Juliet* might fail to carry dramatic weight, might risk not affecting its audience on an emotional level, or might not generate any interest over the story's outcome. Or, in another culture, the ideas of the play might seem so threatening—young couples disobeying their parents—the play would be met by a host of negative reactions, or disbelief.

A director of the play could even change the ideas of *Romeo and Juliet* so they have an outcome and effect entirely different than what it appears Shakespeare intended. Juliet could be played as another young man, or a woman of another race than Romeo. Similarly, a skilled actor might interpret a character in a way that brings out ideas not necessarily apparent in the text. This isn't so much changing a story as bringing to life ideas latent in its text.

Conversely, when actors fail to understand the ideas of a story -- and the dramatic truths of its characters -- they can act—or be directed to act—in a way that brings characters to life, but not in a way that relates to the ideas that other characters represent, or that arise from the story's premise. There's no strong sense of a collective purpose, hence, no strong sense of conflict or drama. The end result is a play or movie that feels muddled or confused about its intentions.

The writer, director, or actor who injects ideas into a story that serve no purpose weakens a story, no matter how insightful their ideas.

The storyteller designing story elements must perceive the quality of movement that those ideas generate. When blocking that movement, the storyteller must choose the ideas that best serve as obstacles to a story's movement. Characters who represent ideas about the power of love in *Romeo and Juliet* are blocked by characters who represent ideas about the power of hate.

In *The Hunt for Red October*, Ramius is aided by characters who believe in the value of freedom. He is oppressed by characters who value a conformity to an idea that generates oppression of others. Therefore, the actions of each set of characters represent these ideas in conflict—freedom versus oppression—brought to life.

Dorothy, in *The Wizard of Oz*, is aided by characters who represent ideas about intelligence, courage, and love. The yellow brick road is symbolic of the idea that life is a journey, and that it is only by making that journey that we discover who we really are.

A simple story might operate with a few ideas plainly on its surface, i.e., good in conflict with evil. A thoughtful story might have characters, events, and actions that represent layers of ideas about life, good, and evil.

The writer who prefers to create a story that operates more purely as a work of ideas must learn to see a story's characters, events, and environment as embodying ideas. Ideas that, because of how they are arranged, create a quality of movement toward an illumination of their dramatic purpose.

A story told through ideas creates characters and events that represent those particular ideas. Through their actions, such characters prove the main dramatic idea at the heart of a story's premise. *Animal Farm*[25] is an example of a story of ideas where characters represent not just themselves, but also ideas about the larger society. A premise for *Animal Farm* could be:

The misuse of power leads to misery and destruction.

Note how the story's dramatic idea revolves around power. Its movement deals with what the misuse of power leads to, and its fulfillment is reflected in the resulting misery and destruction. As the animals' actions shape the outcome of the story's ideas, readers are engaged both emotionally and thoughtfully by the story's fulfillment of its core idea.

Great artists like Joyce, Woolf, Faulkner, and Austen write stories on this dual level of ideas and emotions progressing toward a fulfilling resolution. On the most accessible level, their stories revolve around human needs such as love, hate, the need to matter, redemption, and rebirth. On a deeper level, each artist's unwavering perceptions of life comment on our world and the ideas that underlie the why of our beliefs about love, hate, the need to matter, and so on. Great artists who explore this deeper level through stories have great powers of insight, but their ideas must also revolve around a story premise. Otherwise, their ideas, no matter how brilliant, would fail to create the effect of a story's dramatic movement toward the resolution, fulfillment, and illumination of some facet of the human condition.

What happens when writers confuse ideas with the effect of a story is that they assemble characters who represent ideas. These characters act in clearly symbolic ways. But the actions of the story's characters don't create the effect of a story because they are not arranged to create movement toward illumination.

That fundamental issue of what a story is and how its elements must be arranged to create the effect of a story must be identified and respected. Even when the storyteller's only aim is to create a contest between good and evil in an action film—the story's ideas must be at the service of the story.

What comes first, the story or the idea? My answer is the story. For it an understanding of storytelling that allows storytellers to turn ideas into stories. The storyteller who perceives the relationship of a story's elements to its deepest dramatic issue understands how to blend and arrange his/her story's ideas, character, environment, and events in a satisfactory mix. Every idea can then be used in its rightful place in a story.

Chapter Questions

What do you consider to be the central idea of your story?

How do you introduce the central idea of your story in a dramatic way?

How do the characters of your story embody its ideas?

What would you say is the central idea that embodies your life? Your needs in life?

How does that central idea or those needs impact the types of story ideas you find engaging?

What story ideas affirm your ideas about life?

What story ideas challenge your ideas about life?

Thrust and Counterthrust

When a story begins with events in conflict, characters in collision, ideas challenging each other—it begins a process I call thrust and counterthrust. *Romeo and Juliet* offers an example of this.

The play opens with two kinsmen of the house of Capulet on a street talking about their hatred of the Montagues. Within moments, men of the Montague clan happen by. An insult is hurled, a brawl erupts, members of both clans join in the fray.

This is the first active thrust of the story. It quickly introduces the hatred and feuding between the families. It doesn't *tell* us about their feuding, it acts out the ferocity of the generations-long feud.

Dramatically, this opening thrust leads to the appearance of the Prince of Verona who declares that the next person to break the peace risks death. This is the counterthrust to the brawl.

Another aftermath is that someone asks where Romeo is. His family is concerned for his physical safety. It is revealed that Romeo has been seen alone and obviously unhappy. A clansman is sent to find out why. He finds Romeo, and after some quick probing, discovers he is lovesick over Rosalind. And so we have an answer to the question, what's bothering Romeo? That small thrust of the story is resolved.

The clansman and Romeo come across an unlettered servant who asks Romeo to read an invitation list to a masked ball. Rosalind's name is on the list of the ball being hosted by the Capulets. Romeo, lovesick, ignores the danger and immediately goes to the ball. There he meets Juliet, a Capulet, and falls in love.

That thrust carries the action of the story through to the counterthrust, the complications that ensue from their illicit love.

One sees this process of thrust and counterthrust in the openings of many well-designed stories. For example, *The Wizard of Oz* has Dorothy taking action to save Toto. That thrust of the story takes her into Oz. *Rocky* opens with Rocky being booed in a fight for beating a man after he's down. After the fight, someone yells into his face that Rocky's a bum. That first thrust of the story takes us to a counterthrust, where Rocky is being paid for winning the fight, but most of the money is deducted for various expenses. Rocky's victory is empty.

Lethal Weapon opens with a woman appearing to commit suicide, then moves on to a suicidal detective, Martin Riggs. One thrust—the woman falling or jumping out the window—pulls us into the story's plot. The other thrust pulls us into the story, about whether Riggs will live or die, and why he might choose death.

The Exorcist[26], by William Blatty, opens with a quick thrust: a Jesuit priest realizing that an ancient evil is manifesting itself in the world and that he will be drawn into battling it. It's not a battle that will happen later: it's a battle that is beginning as the story opens. That thrust leads us to the house where the battle will take place.

Funeral For Horses, by Catherine Ryan Hyde, opens with a young woman making a decision to find her missing brother.

The Accidental Tourist[27], by Anne Tyler, opens with Malcom and Sarah driving onto a divided highway as they return early from a vacation meant to rekindle their marriage, which is also heading down a divided highway. The first chapter ends with Sarah asking for a divorce.

The Bad Beginning[28], by Lemony Snicket, opens with the deaths of the parents of the story's three children, Violet, Klaus and Sunny Baudelaire. Then the situation for the children gets infinitely (which in this context means as much as you can imagine and then some) worse.

The first Harry Potter novel, *Harry Potter and the Sorcerer's Stone*[29], opens by setting out the dramatic truth of the Dursley's, that they want above all else to be considered normal, but they have a terrible secret: Mrs. Dursley's sister is a witch, and they loathe witchcraft and how it threatens their sense of mattering. Then, Harry Potter, the son who mysteriously survives the death of his parents at the hands of a powerful wizard, is dropped off at the Dursley's house to be raised in a world of muggles for his own protection.

Each of these storytellers, in describing so clearly the movement of the characters as they act out each story's promise, drew audiences into their worlds.

Writers need to consider if the opening of their stories thrusts it forward in a way that is engaging to an audience. Conversely, if a story doesn't open with some kind of thrust, is there something for the story's characters to respond to. By giving characters something to respond to, they reveal who they are and what drives them.

A story doesn't have to open with a physical thrust. It might open with the thrust of an intriguing idea. The thrust of some state of emotion that calls for explanation and resolution. The thrust of a time and place so unique that an audience wants to know more.

Keep in mind that if by the time you've written your third sentence you aren't three steps into your story, you've given your audience three reasons to set your manuscript aside. That's why publishers, producers, and agents can generally read the first few pages of a manuscript and know if it's something they're going to reject or not. A writer who can't create scenes that dramatically thrust a story forward isn't going to miraculously display that talent on page ten or page one hundred. Yes, by the time most screenplays have gotten to page twenty-five, most novels to page one hundred, and plays to the climax of their first act, the writer's plot devices generally have kicked in and begun supplying momentum to the story. It's just getting past that first twenty-five, forty, or one hundred pages that's an ordeal.

Understanding how to put a story's elements into play with a dramatic thrust on page one is one more tool in the storyteller's tool kit.

Chapter Questions

How does the action of the opening scenes of your story serve to thrust your story forward?

What counterthrust blocks your story's initial forward advance?

Why do your characters perserve when they are blocked?

Writing Dramatic Dialogue

If you want to write tight, spare, evocative dialogue, be clear about what your story is truly about, and what dramatic truths your character's embody. That way you can be sure each character's dialogue acts out your story's promise.

In the beginning of the film *Honey, I Shrunk the Kids*, characters talk about what's at stake with their family breaking up. They also have individual concerns. But what they say always, on some level, ties into the main story issue. Thus, their dialogue moves the story forward.

This is important because a reader or viewer first entering a story wants something that orients him or her. Dialogue that makes clear what's at stake in a story provides this orientation. This is not to suggest characters turn to the reader or viewer and say, "This is what this story's about, this is why I'm here." That's too obvious. Instead, the writer must decide how best to dramatically introduce a story by what characters say and do: that is a part of the writer's craft. To accomplish that dramatic, engaging beginning, a writer can have characters speak to the point of the dramatic purpose in a scene, not away from it.

To understand that process of writing to a dramatic point, consider that you're in a room attending a workshop on writing. A bomb goes off outside the room. Do you continue talking calmly about writing and what brought you to this workshop, or do react in a way that reveals your inner nature?

When characters react to what's at stake in a story as it exerts pressure on them, their actions naturally reveal who they are and how they view their situations. What's at stake in your story might not be as immediate as a bomb blast. It might be a quiet pressure on your characters. But it should still exert some kind of pressure on what your characters say.

Reservoir Dogs[30], by Quentin Tarantino, opens with several armed robbers at a diner making small talk, but the viewers don't know they're armed robbers. In subtle, hip ways, however, the dialogue suggests what's at stake for these ambitious, ruthless men and their sparring to establish dominance in their pack. So when we listen to these men talk, we hear a bomb ticking, even if we don't see it.

For those listening to the opening dialogue of *Reservoir Dogs*, it could be compared to being in a roller coaster car climbing up that first steep hill. Those in the car—the viewers of that opening scene—don't necessarily know what's in store for them. When, at the conclusion of that scene we see that one of these men carries a gun, that roller coaster car we're in hits the last stop before it takes those in the car on a screaming, thrilling ride.

Tarantino, or any storyteller, is the builder of that roller coaster ride. Dialogue that doesn't ring true or that doesn't suggest something is at stake over the outcome of an exchange offers no reason to pay attention; it's the idle chatter of people sitting in a roller coaster car on flat ground, not moving. That kind of experience we can get from life; it's not what people want from a story.

Keep in mind the following to create well-written dialogue.

Consider how people talk when they find themselves in a dramatic, emotional situation. Their dialogue is often short and focused, to the point. Are the people riding in the roller coaster car you've set in motion having relaxed discussions about life when instead they should be screaming or taunting each other or fighting to establish the superiority of their ideas? Or should they be laughing, crying, and holding on to each other for dear life as your story picks up speed and hits a blind turn? Characters' reactions to their environment should be reflected in their dialogue.

When characters are in a dramatic situation, they respond to each other; they are intensely aware of each other's presence.

To create dialogue with "voice," dialogue that feels unique and expressive of each character, avoid packed dialogue. Packed dialogue is dialogue that, to the reader, seems to ask for a response, but none is allowed. An example of packed dialogue:

> BIG MOUTH: "A bomb just went off...I have to call my wife...tomorrow's my birthday and I'll be 41...and this is my first roller coaster ride!"

Note that any one line here calls for a response—if the writer actually was intending there be a conversation. The true purpose of the above dialogue is for the writer to use this character as a mouthpiece to get out information the writer feels is necessary to impart. Such dialogue is flat. It's flat because the only way a character can provide information to the audience is by no longer responding to the situation around him or her. In so doing, the character has detached himself or herself from the story to do the bidding of the writer. The movement of the story at that moment comes to a stop. And if a reader is engaged by your story's movement, you've found a way, only part way through this roller coaster ride, of bringing your story or roller coaster car to a dead stop.

Unpack your dialogue, unless you've packed it for a reason.

Dialogue should advance the story. That means if you have witty, forceful dialogue that doesn't serve some purpose in your story, you're in trouble. In *Last Action Hero*[31], from the time the character Danny is introduced to the moment he enters the movie world of Jack Slater, the dialogue is funny, sharp, witty, clean, terse. But when Danny enters the movie within the movie, the dialogue stops revolving around the point of the story; consequently, it doesn't add anything to the story. Much later in the film, the characters again act and react to the pressures of what's at stake in the story, and all that funny, tight, clean dialogue amounts to something. It advances the story and takes the film into that higher sphere it tried to find by being clever. In order that the stalled roller coaster pick up speed and provide the thrills it initially offered, you should edit out even clever dialogue when it serves no purpose.

Have characters say only what needs to be said. Don't automatically start a scene with characters making introductions unless that serves a dramatic purpose. Don't have characters address each other by name more than once unless you have a reason; repeating of names to no dramatic purpose gets old fast. Also, avoid dialogue that carries a scene to a weak ending. Audiences are very familiar with what needs to be said to move a scene forward. Many writers inadvertently let a scene dribble on with an extra line or two or three. Trust your readers to get the point.

The *Silence of the Lambs*[32] is a movie where the writer paid careful attention to what the actors could communicate with body language. When Clarice Starling enters an elevator with several hulking men, we don't need the writer to tell us out loud about the world she's in. What kind of expectations her character must deal with.

Written English is fundamentally different from spoken English. Oxford Dons speak very correct, formal English, but few others speak that way. I once critiqued a play by an Ethiopian writer and director who had worked as a cab driver in New York. The dialogue of the cab driver characters was strong, barbed, observant, witty. But the writer had his main characters speak a more formal English that robbed them of vitality. I encouraged him to have his main characters speak with the same passion and feeling as his minor characters. Root out written English from your dialogue. It's almost always unnatural and stilted, unless your characters really are Oxford Dons meeting in formal debate. I would suggest, however, that if a bomb went off in the middle of such a debate, it would affect how those Oxford Dons spoke.

Each character should have a personal rhythm for speaking that is a reflection of his or her dramatic truth. This does not mean a writer should load up a character's dialogue with mannerisms as a way to suggest individuality. Too many insincere mannerisms often creates oddly artificial characters. But a dramatic truth should be animating your characters, giving them purpose. That dramatic purpose should be reflected in how characters voice thoughts and feelings.

Avoid having characters be too elusive in their speech. Unless it's well done, it can come across as dramatically flat, or worse, mystifying. Imagine in real life trying to carry on a conversation with someone who never quite gets around to making some clear point. Unless you have a compelling reason to do otherwise, have your characters speak forcefully and directly about what's on their minds, or about what they want the other characters to think is on their minds. Once they've said what's on their minds, have other characters respond in a direct fashion.

Trust your actors. In a film or play script, actors are trained to express feelings and moods with body language. Many beginning writers load their scripts and plays with reams of unnecessary dialogue to convey information that could be acted out.

If your characters don't have strong feelings that compel them to speak out about what's happening around them, why are they in your story? Unless they care about something or have something at stake that compels them to speak out, edit them out.

Finally, individual characters should have different tones of voice during the events of a story. An angry man will talk one way to his boss, another to his wife, another to his son, and still another to his daughter. A character with a sad voice might be elevated to a triumphant voice at the climax of your story. To have a character with only a single note "voice," no matter the circumstances of a story, is most often to have created a plot device for the use of the writer. When all the characters in a story have the same voice, they are extentions of the author and lack their own dramatic truths.

A plot that heightens and makes visible what's at stake in a story, and that sets out dramatically which characters are achieving goals and which are losing out, allows characters to travel through various states of emotion—from anger to pain to ecstasy to grief to jubilation. The climax comes when the characters develop a different sense of themselves, a new voice.

Keep in mind when you write dialogue that actors love roles that give them a chance to play strong, dramatic characters. They want to feel pride in their work, be recognized for their craft. Even if you're writing a low-budget action adventure movie, you should understand what your story is about. Write tight, clean dialogue that gives your actors a chance to show what they can do. They'll appreciate you.

If you're struggling with writing strong dialogue, remember the axiom about the three things that sell real estate: location, location, location. If you're struggling to write powerful dialogue, keep in mind the three main principles of writing powerful dialogue: reactions, reactions, reactions. Let your characters react to each other. Let loose with what they think and feel in a direct, forceful way that compels a response.

If you're writing scripts for a particular genre, action-adventure or romantic comedy for example, watch a movie in that genre. Pay close attention to how many exchanges of dialogue happen in individual scenes. Watch how the actors use body language to communicate information. Turn the sound off if that's what you need to do to see what's happening on the screen. Learn to see the story as it's told via visual images; don't get lulled into being a passive viewer who creates passive characters who tell each other the meaning of everything. As a writer, it's your job to dramatically shape the material that others will view.

Study movies, watch plays, take an acting class, even write a one-act play and direct it yourself as a staged reading for the public. Actors love to work with fresh material. Finding actors, even in small communities, is usually never more than a few phone calls away. Directing your own one act play can teach you volumes about dialogue. Are you overlaying your feelings on a scene? Direct it for the 20th time: you'll start to hear if the dialogue in the scene is alive and fresh. Well written-dialogue holds up over time. Weak dialogue very quickly grates on the ears.

Do your actors stumble over the same lines again and again? Rewrite them. Listen to your actors when they tell you a line doesn't ring true, or is difficult to say. If you can't find actors, ask a friend to help you read the dialogue from your script out loud. If you don't have a friend to help, do it yourself and record it, then play it back and listen to it. You're competing against people who will take the time to make their dialogue tight and clean.

If you want to write an action novel, read a popular action novel and see how the author handles dialogue.

Well written dialogue invites readers and viewers into your story by promising them that what they'll hear has dramatic meaning and purpose.

Chapter Exercises

Write a scene with two characters who say something concrete about their dramatic truths in five words or less. Write five exchanges of dialogue, with each character saying something to the other about his or her dramatic truth that provokes a response.

Write a scene with two characters who express anger. Write five exchanges. Keep each expression under ten words.

Write a scene with the same two characters sharing their true feelings toward each other for the first time. Again, keep the exchanges brief, under ten words.

Create characters who have opposing dramatic truths, and put them into a room in a situation where both characters want something, but only one person can leave that room with what they both desire.

Write a scene with five exchanges of dialogue. Have two characters interrupt each other and not allow the other to finish a thought because each is so excited about what they are talking about.

SECTION THREE

OUTLINING YOUR STORY

Story Line and Plot Line

Being able to diagram the key elements of a story provides a foundation for understanding the relationship between those elements. The outline process starts with an understanding of what a story, story line, and plot line are, and the distinctions between the three.

Story—an arrangement of words, images, or sounds that promise to take an audience on a purposeful, dramatic journey.

Plot—the events that heighten a story's dramatic impact by blocking a story's advance toward resolution. Plot events are designed to strike story characters in a manner that compels more potent and deeper revelations about why characters feel a need to shape what's at stake in a story, and to compel characters to take action.

Story line—the events that set out a story introduction and advance toward the resolution and fulfillment of a story's promise in a way discernible and compelling to a story's audience.

Plot line—the events that make a story's advance along its story line dramatic and compelling for both a story's characters and its audience.

Understanding how a story, its story line and plot line operate together offers a clear view into how a story can be designed to move an audience emotionally or thoughtfully.

To show how story, story line and plot line interact, page seventy-eight has a diagram of a story and its story and plot lines. Note how the story's plot escalates (heightens) the drama over the story's advance.

To demonstrate the distinction between story, story line, and plot line, I'll use the premise for *Romeo and Juliet*.

The premise of this story is: Great love defies even death.

(continued on page 77)

Story Line/Plot Line Diagram

Original graphic design: Bill Johnson
Additional graphic design: Lawrence Booth

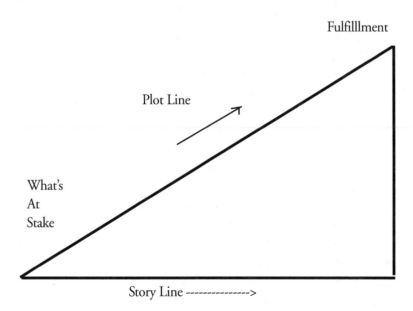

Because this story's premise identifies its key dramatic issue, it is the place to find the answer to the question, what is this story about? It's about *love*.

It's that simple, at least on the surface. What often leads people away from focusing on this simple look into the heart of a story is the natural human desire to *explain* a story with a presentation of facts about plot events and characters, rather than considering how to evoke the journey a story offers (here, a story about grand, passionate love). Explaining the history of the feud that keeps Romeo and Juliet apart doesn't convey the very real, very human passions that the story explores.

To begin this process of understanding how to make a distinction between a story, its story line, and plot line, start with the simple answer to the question: what kind of love does this story explore? A love willing to defy all that stands in its way. A simple answer, which comes out of the premise. It speaks to how this issue plays out dramatically in this particular story.

How does this story manifest the fulfillment of its dramatic issue of its characters being willing to defy everything that stands between them? In this story, they begin by defying their parents and, ultimately, defying death itself. By defying death to be together, Romeo and Juliet prove the greatness of their love.

Again, this is an answer that comes out of the story's premise. It is an answer, not an explanation, of what the story's about. Just as writing the word fire doesn't evoke heat, simply writing the words "great love" doesn't evoke that experience for an audience. An audience must be moved emotionally and thoughtfully to experience this great love.

Charting a story's advance toward resolution and fulfillment helps a writer perceive the story's advance along its story line.

At its most basic, the story line in a story about love could be described as: The *beginning* of this story line sets out that this is a story about love.

One should *start* with this answer to avoid becoming lost in a maze of character and plot issues. The storyteller should be aware of *why* the beginning of a story is its beginning, and not something else, i.e., an introduction of characters, or a plot-event, or a description of an environment.

The *middle* of the story line is the complications that ensue when characters seeking to prove their love must find a way to be together in spite of escalating obstacles.

This description of the middle of the story line creates for a storyteller a clear view of this story's advance and the kind of complications that threaten to block that advance.

The *conclusion* or *fulfillment* of the story and its story line is that by defying all the obstacles, the power of great love is demonstrated in a tragic, fulfilling way.

As communicated in this simple story line, there is an introduction of the story's promise, complications, and an escalation of drama around what must happen to advance the story dramatically. And, finally, fulfillment of the promise. A beginning, middle, and end.

Any event or character that doesn't tie into that story line and serve some purpose in bringing this story to life is dramatically irrelevant or inert.

You can test whether characters have an effect on a story by either removing them or replacing them with a different character, an old man replacing a young boy, for example. If nothing in the story changes in a material way, those characters are dramatically inert.

Just as a story has a story line, it also has a plot line. As a story's events advance the story along its story line, the events on the plot line operate to dramatically heighten that advance.

To talk about the plot line of *Romeo and Juliet* is to ask: What *events* manifest or make visible the dramatic introduction of this story about love?

In this story, characters who are emotionally designed to have issues around love are placed into situations that test and challenge their willingness to prove their love. Thus, they feel compelled by the story's plot events to react. And, their actions in turn advance the story along both its plot and story lines.

This plot line is composed of those events that resolve and fulfill that the love in this story has, in fact, defied all the obstacles in its path.

Events that show the story's main characters proving their love by dramatically defying all obstacles in their path, including death. Those are the events that advance the story along its plot line.

The events on a story's plot line should be designed to impact a story's characters in a way that they offer revelations about their feelings and about what drives them. Because a story's plot events strike at a story's characters with more and more force, a story's characters react with new feelings, offer new revelations, and come to new understandings, all of which help the audience track a story's movement along its story line.

Note that in this discussion of a story, plot, story line, and plot line about love proving itself great, I do not need to mention a particular character, his or her goals, or a story's events. Once writers have a foundation of understanding a story, plot, story line, and plot line, how they interweave, and what that effect generates for an audience, they have a stronger foundation for understanding what types of characters and events best tell a story. Storytellers who understand the foundation of a story have more confidence that they are telling a dramatic, moving story, and not simply offering more and more details about things that fail to engage an audience.

To demonstrate the connection between story, plot, and characters, I'll return to *Romeo and Juliet*.

In *Romeo and Juliet*, we're introduced to characters who have issues of proving their love. As the story opens, they have internal conflicts revolving around love. They are interacting with other characters who also have issues of love and hate to resolve, and all the story's characters are in an environment—a lethal feud between their families—that keeps them apart.

These characters are emotionally ripe. Because they are *designed* to react when challenged. Their reactions advance the story along its story line when another character or event blocks them. Their reactions to the obstacles allow the story's audience to track the story's advance.

For example, the story opens with a brawl between the two clans which shows the depth of the hate that will block Romeo and Juliet. We're then quickly introduced to Romeo, a young man in love with the idea of love. The story question that arises is: Will Romeo's desire to find a young woman to whom he can speak of his love be fulfilled?

The scene question is: Who will be exiled if there's any more public brawling and mayhem?

It is the purpose of the plot to make this last question dramatic, for in its answer lies the story's resolution and fulfillment. So the events that the *plot* sets in motion—the lethal feud, Romeo meeting Juliet—advance the story along both its *plot* line and *story* line.

By learning what roots characters in the deeper issue of a story, a storyteller can learn to create more potent plot events that are clearly in the service of a story.

Writers who are unable to make a distinction between a story, story line, and plot line, often create stories that have a strong plot lines—this happened, so consequently that happened—but a weak story line. Things happen, but it doesn't mean much to the story's audience, because the audience hasn't been led to feel emotionally or thoughtfully engaged by a story's events and character goals. The revelations generated by a story's plot don't clearly advance the story along its story line, because there often is no clear, discernible introduction of a story issue. Plot events not rooted in a deeper story issue don't strike characters

79

in a way that elicits deeper, more potent truths as a story advances, because no story context has been established to what characters clearly want.

To ensure that your story is advancing dramatically, identify how each scene or chapter is a clearly defined step. Are you suggesting the beginning of that step in an opening scene? Is the closing scene of a chapter an affirmation that a step has been taken, and that the completion of that step requires a second step that will be the basis of a next chapter/step?

If you have trouble understanding this, break down a Harry Potter novel. They are very mechanical in terms of how they advance, in how they set up a concrete step for each chapter, and end with a resolution that raises a question for the next chapter to answer.

A well-designed story line generates vivid, passionate characters acting with clear purpose; a story without a clearly evoked story line creates a row of mannequins awkwardly moved around the story's stage by its author. That's why writers who write plots devoid of issues of human need struggle to bring their characters and plots to life, just as dressing a mannequin in fancy clothes and putting it in a sports car with James Bond does not bring it to life.

Chapter Questions

Without mentioning your characters, can you write a simple story line for your story?

Can you write a simple plot line?

How do the events of your plot compel your characters to speak deeper truths about themselves, offering more potent revelations that resonate with your audience?

Do you understand how your characters advance your story along your story line?

Using Story Director^(TM) to Outline Your Story

The ability to understand the dramatic purpose of every element of a story is an important tool. The Story Director process is meant to help writers check whether or not every event, character action, and plot device serves to dramatically advance a story toward the resolution and fulfillment of its promise.

Story Director can be used before a story is written or after a story is written, to ensure a story has a strong foundation to build on. I've found that many, many writers have to write a story before they understand the issues at its heart.

Story Director could be used as a starting point for a writer to ask some general questions about a story, or to discuss a story with other writers.

I understand there is no one-size-fits-all way of understanding how to tell a story, or to break out the elements of a story. I came up with the Story Director process to help struggling storytellers have a clearer sense of why their stories are dramatically unfocused, or not quite engaging or rewarding. The only method I've found that truly helps such writers is to teach them how to consciously understand how to tell a story and design its elements. Once they integrate that knowledge, they can then focus their energy and imagination on telling a story, instead of circling around new plot designs and character traits to find a way to bring a story to life.

As such, Story Director is not meant to be a quick fix. It's meant to deepen the understanding of storytellers in a way that transforms their writing.

To illustrate and demonstrate the Story Director process, this chapter includes a story diagram that outlines the dramatic elements of *The Hunt for Red October*. Following the steps in this chapter will help writers create a similar diagram for their stories.

The objective of setting out the steps for outlining a story is:

It helps writers identify the issues that make for a well-told story: compelling story promise, dynamic premise, clear introduction of a story's promise, engaging characters acting out that promise, strong conflict, dramatic plot, vivid fulfillment, clearly defined dramatic truths.

It helps writers to see how a story is more than a sequential arrangement of events. It's a process whereby the story moves toward a dramatic state of resolution and fulfillment that the audience can share.

It helps a storyteller perceive the process of setting in motion a dramatic story, so a story can begin with a strong foundation.

Each section of Story Director has a subheading, subject title, and questions you should be answering in order to create a story diagram. There are also suggestions for what answers might look like using *The Hunt for Red October* as an example. There is no single right or wrong answer to any of the questions. The questions are meant to ask you to think about particular story issues, and to consider what the answers to the questions might be.

Premise

To start the outline process, write your premise across the bottom of a piece of paper, laid out horizontally (see diagram, page 92).

If you're having trouble creating a premise, refer to the chapter on techniques for creating a story premise.

The premise for *The Hunt for Red October* is:

The courage to battle oppression leads to freedom.

The next step is to identify what's at stake in your story. What's at stake in *The Hunt for Red October* is whether the values of democracy are stronger than the values of oppression.

Finish this sentence:

What's at stake in my story is...

If you're still having trouble identifying what's at stake in your story, re-read the chapter about that process.

Creating a Story Question

Once you are clear about what's at stake in your story, phrase that issue as a story question. This story question is then answered by the action of the story's events, characters, plot devices, arrangement of ideas, etc. For example, in *The Hunt for Red October*, what's at stake is the outcome of this battle between freedom and oppression. This conflict is initiated and acted out through Ramius, who seeks to escape to America. If Ramius can escape to America and gain his freedom, the values of freedom are proven to be stronger than oppression.

The story question that arises from what's at stake in the story is: Can Ramius escape to America and gain his freedom?

You have to read to the end of the story to find the dramatic answer to that question. While a story question typically refers to the story's main character and his or her goals, this question is rooted in what's at stake in the story.

For the purpose of creating this particular story, its conflict is presented as a question, not a statement. The forces of oppression must appear *able* to defeat Ramius and the values of freedom, otherwise the story generates no drama over its outcome.

To set out your story question, finish this sentence:

> *The main dramatic question that arises from what's at stake in my story is…*

Put your one sentence story question just below your premise.

Story Line

The story line for *The Hunt for Red October* is represented on the diagram as a line above the premise.

Write a one-paragraph story line for your story. A story line for *The Hunt for Red October* could be written as:

> *The Hunt for Red October* is one man's quest to be free of the system that oppresses him. To gain his freedom, Ramius, the commander of a Soviet, advanced propulsion, nuclear-missile submarine, sets into motion a plan to escape to America. His daring attempt to escape quickly becomes known, and his oppressors hunt Ramius with all the forces at

their command. By bringing to bear the full weight of the Soviet Navy to stop Ramius, the American Navy and government are alerted to the fact that a rogue Soviet submarine—armed with nuclear missiles—is approaching America. Is it commanded by a madman who must be destroyed? Or a man who loves freedom and is attempting to escape his oppressors? Jack Ryan, a CIA analyst, intuitively understands what compels Ramius. Because Ryan operates in a free society, his opinion is heard. In a daring rescue, Ryan boards the *Red October* and helps Ramius escape to America…and freedom.

The purpose of writing out the story line is for storytellers to be clear that every element of a story serves to advance it toward its resolution and fulfillment.

The beginning of this story is: Ramius taking action to gain his freedom.

The middle of the story line is: The complications around Ramius gaining his freedom.

The end of the story line is: Ramius gaining his freedom.

Draw a straight line above your story question to represent your story line. Every element of your story should advance it along this line.

Plot Line

A plot line describes a story in terms of its plot. Just as a story has a beginning, middle, and end, its plot also has a beginning, middle, and end. The interweaving of a story's plot events with the events on a story line dramatically advances a story.

A plot line for *The Hunt for Red October* could read:

The Hunt for Red October is a story about the conflict between freedom and oppression. Ramius, the commander of a Soviet, advanced propulsion nuclear submarine, commandeers the submarine in an attempt to flee to freedom in America. To set in motion his plan, Ramius kills the ship's political officer. From that point, he must either succeed in his quest or die. Next, Ramius eludes other Soviet submarines sent to find him. Later, he eludes both the Soviet and U.S. Navies. Both the Soviets and U.S. fear what a rogue commander of a nuclear-missile submarine might do. In the U.S., Jack Ryan, a CIA analyst, intuits that Ramius intends to escape to America to be free. Because Ryan operates in a free system, others heed his counsel. Through his heroism and

Ramius's undeniable desire to be free, Ramius escapes to America in the *Red October*. In a highly dramatic climax, Ryan and Ramius outwit Ramius's communist oppressors. Ramius is free at last.

Note that this plot line identifies the obstacles that block Ramius. Because they block Ramius, they heighten the drama over the story's outcome. That escalation of the story's drama is the purpose of the obstacles.

Write a one-paragraph description of your story's plot line. Begin with the statement:

The plot line of my story is...

In your plot outline, identify what obstacles block the movement of your story.

To help you identify those obstacles, answer the following question: The obstacles that block my main character achieving his or her goals are...

As your main character seeks to attain goals, the story's plot should *escalate* the obstacles that block that character's movement. To help you verbalize this process, finish the following sentence: The plot of my story escalates the obstacles my main character must overcome by...

On the story diagram, as Ramius acts to overcome the obstacles blocking his gaining freedom, the story not only advances but also increases in dramatic intensity. If the obstacles that block the movement of your story do not lead to this escalation in dramatic tension, you're running the risk of creating a story that is a series of events.

How to Start Your Story on Page One

What do you write to set your story into action on page one? There is probably no single question that more bedevils inexperienced writers. To discover the answer, consider these story openings:

Rocky, a story about self-respect, opens with Rocky being called a bum. This sets the *story* into motion because the story is about what Rocky must do to gain self-respect. A scene showing the little sense of self worth he has being battered sets this story into motion.

A Christmas Carol opens by showing us the degree to which Scrooge has become an embittered crust of a human being, seemingly beyond redemption or renewal. That raises a question: Can Scrooge be renewed?

Pride and Prejudice[33], by Jane Austin, introduces two characters who seem made for each other...except for their issues of pride and prejudice. Can they overcome those issues to be together?

By identifying what's at stake in your story and creating characters and events in need of resolution, you set your story into motion from its opening lines.

How you set out what's at stake in your story—in a manner subtle or blunt, through physical action, emotions in transition, a declaration of thoughts—is a personal preference.

Only when what's at stake in your story is clearly communicated to your audience can your audience assign meaning to the actions of your characters.

If your audience has to wait forty pages to discover that Ramius plans to escape the system that oppresses him to gain his freedom, your story starts on page forty-one.

In answering the question of what it is that sets your story in motion on page one, answer the following:

The dramatic issue at the heart of my story is...
(Character name) is my main character because his or her actions manifest the movement of my story by...

In *The Hunt for Red October*, the dramatic issue at the heart of the story is the conflict between the values of and the conflict between freedom and oppression. Ramius manifests this conflict as he sets in motion his plan to fight the oppressive system that denies him his freedom.

Now, finish the following:

My opening scene sets my story about courage, renewal, rebirth, etc. into motion on page one by...

In *The Hunt for Red October,* Ramius sets the story into motion by killing the ship's political officer and mailing a letter to Moscow stating his intentions. From that point on, he has no choice but to either gain his freedom or die.

Plot Questions

Once writers can communicate a story line and plot line for their stories, they can set out the elements or events of their plots in relationship to their stories. Again, a plot should be recognized as an aspect of a story's movement.

The story of *The Hunt for Red October* is about the battle between freedom and oppression. While the story has an overall story question, it also has an ongoing series of questions raised during the course of the story. Some of these questions might be raised at the beginning of a chapter, and resolved within that chapter. The chapter question that arises in Chapter One of *The Hunt for Red October* is: Will Ramius be able to overcome the political officer on board the submarine? He must be able to overcome the political officer before his plan to escape can proceed. Note how the issue is raised as a question. Since it's raised as a question that is tied to the deeper purpose of the story—the political oficer is Ramius's oppressor in residence—the question is enmeshed in what's at stake in the story. By developing drama around the answer to this particular question and resolving it, the story moves forward.

What question, based on what's at stake in your story, do you set up in your first ten pages? In one sentence, explain how that question arises from what's at stake in your story. The first obstacle that my main character must confront and overcome is…

While Ramius is the story's primary character and instigator of its action, all the characters in the story have roles to play. Their actions serve to either advance the story, or, by blocking its movement, to escalate the drama over its outcome.

To fit the story diagram onto a single page, I have limited the chapter questions to the most prominent. Every chapter of your book should generate drama over its outcome.

In *The Hunt for Red October,* the first obstacle that Ramius must overcome is the political officer. It is marked with a question mark on the diagram. To be dramatic, the outcome of the scene should be in doubt.

Story and Characters

The story outline refers to those characters—or groups of characters—who have the most significant impact on shaping the course and outcome of the story: the American Navy, the Soviet Navy, the American government, the Soviet government, Jack Ryan, the KGB assassin.

Answer the following:

> *In my story about (character name), my main character feels compelled to act because...*
> *The dramatic purpose of the character who opposes my main character is...*

Every character in a story should have a discernible dramatic purpose the storyteller can identify. For example, the characters who oppose Ramius are in the service of the system that oppresses him.

For *The Hunt for Red October,* Ramius feels compelled to challenge the system that oppresses him because it has led to the death of his wife and the destruction of his homeland. The characters who oppose Ramius are his communist overseers, the military they command, and, initially, the American military.

Story and Drama

To understand how a particular story both advances toward resolution and transports and audience toward a story's fulfillment is to perceive that creating drama in a story requires blocking that advance. For example, in *The Hunt for Red October*, the story is about freedom battling oppression. What blocks this story's movement of Ramius seeking to gain his freedom? An escalation of oppression.

This story *starts* not with Ramius thinking about or creating his plans, but *acting*—moving—on them. Since his actions advance the story, the story starts on page one.

Write down in your story notes:

> *The movement of my story about... will be blocked by...*

In *The Hunt for Red October,* the advance of this story about freedom in conflict with oppression is blocked by the military might of the oppressive communist system, and an assassin aboard the *Red October*. Ramius is blocked in his attempt to gain his freedom by the military might of the communist Soviet Union and an assassin in their employ.

What kind of characters will block the advance of Ramius toward achieving this state of freedom? Those who are powerful and fear-inspiring.

Write in your notes:

The characters who will block my story's advance are...

In *The Hunt for Red October,* the characters who move to block Ramius are the ship's political officer, the Soviet military, and a KGB assassin. They have dramatic truths that are in opposition to what Ramius believes.

Conflict

It is a hallmark of a well-told story that its conflict escalates the drama over its outcome.

By binding together every character, a story's premise ensures that when characters act, they find themselves in conflict with other characters. Because only one person or group can shape the outcome over what's at stake in the story, this generates conflict.

For your outline notes, finish the following:

The characters in my story are in conflict over what's at stake in it because...
They feel compelled to resolve this issue no matter what price they must pay because...
The following actions and events make visible and concrete my story's conflict...
The following actions by my story's characters escalate the level of conflict in my story by...

Stories and Ideas

Using *The Hunt for Red October* as an example, we see that this is a story not just about a clash between characters who value freedom, but also about a clash of ideas: Which type of political system is better, Communism or Democracy?

While this story is primarily action-oriented, the ideas in play also arise from its premise. This is a vital issue because inexperienced storytellers can come to believe that a story *is* an idea. I argue, however, that an idea might be at the root of a story, but a story is an arrangement of ideas, issues, events, characters, and plot devices for a particular purpose: the dramatic enactment of an issue of human need to a resolution and fulfillment an audience shares.

Finish the following:

The main idea at the heart of my story is...

The idea at dramatic play in *The Hunt for Red October* is whether the values of democracy are stronger than the values of communism.

Drama

Because the issue at stake in the story is raised as a question, the storyteller generates drama over its outcome. The more drama a story generates, the more the storyteller creates the effect of a page-turner (a novel an audience can't put down). A story must develop drama to communicate that what's at stake has enough value that its characters are willing to engage in conflict to shape a story's course and outcome.

Finish this sentence:

The drama in my story is generated by...

The drama in *The Hunt for Red October* arises from a clearly established conflict between freedom and oppression, that the audience is led to internalize through the actions of the story's characters.

Story Complications

Remember, whether your story is about courage, love, or a desire to be important, the plot should raise obstacles to be overcome. Characters must act with ever greater action to move the story forward. During this period of your story, how does the drama over your story's outcome escalate?

The purpose of putting your characters in a position where they *must* act with force and strength of emotion is so your audience experiences those states of potent action and feeling.

In your story outline, write:

By creating the following obstacles with the plot, my protagonist and those who aid the protagonist, will be driven to stronger and stronger actions...

Ramius is driven to act with more and more determination because of the escalating steps the communists and their military forces take to stop him.

Complications

In a typical American commercial film, the story's characters reach a point where it seems courage will be defeated, that love will not prevail, that the ruthless and oppressive will overcome the noble and heroic. In his analysis of story structure, Syd Field calls this plot-point two in his book *Screenplay: Foundation of Screenwriting*[34].

Considering plot-point two from the perspective of how the arrangement of a story's elements operate to create movement toward resolution and fulfillment, it signifies a story has moved to a state of events where those who have internalized the story most deeply fear or feel anxious that the story will not be fulfilled or resolved in a favorable way. The storyteller creates this effect for the very purpose of making a particular story's fulfillment (for example, that courage does win the day, love does prevail, the noble person does overcome the unjust) that's much more potent and dramatic to an audience.

For your story outline, finish the following:

> *At this point, all seems lost to my main character because…*

In *The Hunt for Red October,* all seems lost when it appears the assassin will kill Ramius.

Fulfillment

Moving past the point where all seems lost, a story can move ahead to its fulfillment. In a story about courage, this is when courage wins the day. It is when, through the actions of the story's characters, the story's premise is fulfilled.

For this part of your outline, finish the following:

> *The fulfillment of my story is…*
> *The fulfillment of my story is made visible and concrete by the actions of the story's characters as they accomplish…*

A distinction must be made here between the resolution of character goals and the fulfillment of a story. As a character's goals are resolved in a story's climax, the action of the story's plot is resolved. But it is by the action of the story's characters to resolve a story's premise that the story itself is fulfilled. That's why I say that the fulfillment of the story and the climax of its plot are two separate issues.

Now, at the end of this outline, look again at your story premise. Did the elements of your story serve that premise? During the process of creating the outline, you might discover you had a different premise in mind. It is the purpose of the outline to help you resolve that kind of problem.

The fulfillment of *The Hunt for Red October* is that Ramius gains his freedom. The story's fulfillment is made visible and concrete by Ramius not only gaining his freedom, but also by the Americans finding a way to keep the *Red October*.

Diagram

Now that you've created a story outline, you should have something that looks like the following diagram.

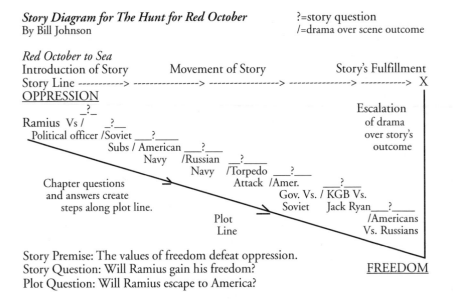

Story Diagram for The Hunt for Red October
By Bill Johnson

?=story question
/=drama over scene outcome

Red October to Sea
Introduction of Story   Movement of Story   Story's Fulfillment
Story Line ------------> ----------------> ------------------> ----------------> -----------> X
OPPRESSION
        ?   Escalation
      _:_   of drama
Ramius Vs /   _?__   over story's
 Political officer /Soviet ___?____   outcome
      Subs / American ___?___
         Navy   /Russian   __?____
              Navy /Torpedo ___?___
   Chapter questions   Attack /Amer.   ___?___
   and answers create   Gov. Vs. / KGB Vs.
     steps along plot line.   Soviet   Jack Ryan___?____
                    Plot   /Americans
                    Line   Vs. Russians

Story Premise: The values of freedom defeat oppression.
Story Question: Will Ramius gain his freedom?   FREEDOM
Plot Question: Will Ramius escape to America?

Summary

Now that you have an outline and notes for your story, my last questions for you are: Does your story question arise from what's at stake in your story? Does what's at stake in your story arise from your premise? Do the opening scenes of your story introduce your main character and his or her issues and goals in a way that makes clear the connection to what's at stake in your story? Do you see how creating a series of questions around resolving issues and events draws your audience through your story to experience its resolution and fulfillment? Do the obstacles that block the movement of your story operate to escalate the drama over your story's outcome? Do the events mentioned in your story line and in your plot line interweave in a way that together they operate to advance your story toward its resolution and fulfillment? Does the action of your story dramatically introduce, resolve, and fulfill your story's promise? Fulfill your character's dramatic truths?

The purpose of this outline process is to enable you to answer these questions *before* you begin writing.

If it's difficult for you to work through the sequence of your story before you write it, some writers set out story, plot, character issues, and ideas on 3 x 5 cards that can be easily rearranged. You can write ideas for scenes on individual cards, develop interesting character issues, and think up bits of dialogue as it comes to you, without feeling like you're making a commitment to any particular idea, event or character action. For some people, this process helps free their creative imagination. Once you've collected a number of scenes, you might then use the outline process to give them a sense of dramatic order. Or, it might work best for you to write a complete draft of your screenplay, novel, or play, then use the outline process to help you with rewrites.

Some screenwriting programs allow writers to create outline notes alongside a script, or incorporate notes into a script.

If you're writing alone and you need some outside stimulation or probing questions to get you thinking about a story in a new light, there are computer programs, books, and audio tapes available to help you.

The Story Director™ outline process is designed to guide writers to see clearly what the promise of their story is, to perceive what *questions* arise from a story's promise being acted out, to understand what sets a story into *motion* from its opening lines, to perceive which details most clearly and potently evoke the *movement* of a story, to understand how to *transfer* the tension over a story's course and outcome from a story's *characters* to its *audience*, and to perceive what kind of fulfillment will offer an audience *relief* from the tensions generated by a well-told story.

The overall goal here is to help writers better understand how the elements of a story interweave to create the effect of a well-told story. Once writers learn how to outline a story, they can begin a particular story with an understanding of how best to dramatically set out its elements. The result is a story that starts from a solid foundation, instead of a story that never quite overcomes a weak beginning. Just as important, a story designed to open with a strong, clear dramatic focus communicates to its audience that this is a story world created by someone who understands the art of storytelling.

Such stories naturally draw in and sustain the attention of an audience.

The ability to understand *what* words, *which* images, *which* characters, *what* dialogue, and *which* events most dramatically set a story into motion around resolving its promise is at the heart of the art of storytelling.

Chapter Questions

Did creating the diagram help you see how your story line and plot line work together?

Did it help you see the process of thrust and counter-thrust in your story?

Did it help you to see how your story line and plot line should interweave?

Do you need a larger drawing surface? Some people lay out butcher paper over the top of a table or counter, or tack it up against a wall so they can see the progression of a story and add notes as they have new ideas. Others write down scene, plot or character ideas on three by five cards, one idea to a card, then put the cards into some kind of order. Use the outline system that helps you the most.

Writing Out a Story's Spine

Writing one page that reflects the spine of a story -- the central issue resolved by a main character, can greatly help in the creation of a one page synopsis. Understanding a story's spine is also valuable when describing a story to agents, producers, and editors.

Many writers struggle with writing out a story's spine because they want to set out the actions of their characters and plot. To describe a story, however, is a separate issue from writing about a character's goals or one's plot. For example, the story of *The Hunt for Red October* is about freedom battling oppression.

To describe *The Hunt for Red October*, then, is not the same as talking about the actions of its main character, Ramius.

A story spine for The Hunt for Red October *might begin: This is the story of one man's battle to be free of the system that oppresses him.*

Note, the first line identifies what's at stake in the story, namely freedom battling oppression.

One should avoid writing: The Hunt for Red October is the story of Ramius, the commander of a Soviet, nuclear-missile submarine who uses the submarine too flee to America.

Ramius acts out the story issue of a man who will not be denied his freedom, but the story itself is about this issue of freedom battling oppression.

The story's spine should make clear what's at stake in the story itself. To continue:

To gain his freedom, Ramius, the commander of the Soviet, nuclear-missile submarine Red October, *sets in motion a plan to escape to America.*

Note that Ramius is described in relationship to what's at stake in the story, the issue of freedom. This continues the spine describing the issue that underlies the story itself.

> One should avoid writing: As the story opens, Ramius, commander of the nuclear-missile armed submarine Red October, sets in motion a plan to escape to America.

This only offers a description of the story's main character and the story's plot. It doesn't suggest the connection between Ramius's actions, the story's plot, and what's at stake in the story.

> *Ramius has long hated his oppressors, the communist party that rules Russia and his native Lithuania. He's been held in check while his wife was alive. With her passing, he has no restraints on his desire to be free.*

This gives a sense of why Ramius desires to be free: it is to escape the oppression of his communist masters, whom he loathes. Even though this appears to be describing Ramius, it's describing him in a way that makes clear his relationship to the story itself.

> One should avoid writing: Ramius wants to pay back the communists for what they have done to Lithuania, his homeland.

This explains why Ramius acts, and although it's true, it doesn't tie his actions into the story's underlying premise.

> *To set in motion his plot to escape to America and freedom, Ramius must risk killing his political officer. Then he gives his crew orders that they must follow blindly, because he's the ship's captain. Ramius knows one of the crew has been trained to kill him if he acts suspiciously.*

This description continues to tie Ramius's actions into the story's underlying premise, that he can act to gain his freedom but must take risks. It is the nature of a story that the actions of a story's characters and its plot generate drama over its outcome. A story spine should offer an idea about a story's drama. Because Ramius is part of an oppressive system, it is guaranteed that his orders will be obeyed. This description of the story ties these elements into its premise. The story spine raises a dramatic issue that plays throughout the story. How long can Ramius hide his true purpose from his assassin?

> Avoid writing: Ramius kills the Red October's political officer, and then gives his crew orders he knows they will follow because he's

the ship's captain.

The above merely describes the actions of Ramius without tying them into the story's underlying premise or without giving a strong suggestion of the drama over the story's course and outcome.

> *Killing the political officer is only a first step. Next, Ramius must avoid detection by his fellow submariners when they are ordered to find and detain him. Later, to find and destroy him. His communist oppressors fear what a free man armed with nuclear missiles might do.*

Note the repetition of the story's main theme, freedom, and the escalation of the drama over the story's outcome. Ramius's oppressors now actively hunt him. Note how this story spine shows that with each step Ramius moves toward freedom, while others double their efforts to stop him. This, in brief, is the purpose of the story's plot, to increase the drama over the story's outcome.

Avoid writing: Ramius outmaneuvers the Soviet submarines sent to find him, captained by men he has trained. In Moscow, those in the military and communist party begin to fear what Ramius might be planning, and plot his destruction.

The above fails to directly state "why" the men in Moscow fear Ramius.

> *Ramius' outmaneuvering of the Soviet submarine fleet alerts the Soviet surface navy to find and destroy him. The Soviet navy going on alert in the Atlantic puts the Americans on the alert. When they learn that a nuclear-armed submarine is on a course toward America, decisions must be made about the nature of the Soviet threat. If the* Red October *is a rogue submarine, the Americans will destroy it. Tensions escalate in Washington, D.C. and Moscow. CIA analyst Jack Ryan suspects Ramius's true purpose.*

Note how this introduces Jack Ryan, the other main character of the story. His actions revolve around the idea that Jack is listened to because he operates in a free system. This description of Jack ties his actions into the story's underlying premise.

Avoid writing: Ramius, outmaneuvering the Soviet submarine fleet, finds the Soviet Atlantic fleet on full alert with intentions to find and destroy him. An American attack submarine that has picked up

Ramius's trail passes along information about the Red October. The American sailors are intelligent, capable, and able to think for themselves, in contrast to their Soviet counterparts. In Washington, D.C., CIA analyst Jack Ryan suspects that Ramius's purpose may not be what it appears. He is a strong, charismatic man, and his opinion is listened to. In Washington and Moscow, tensions mount.

The above is okay, but it doesn't clearly identify what's at stake in the story.

Ramius and the *Red October* narrowly avoid being destroyed by a Soviet attack submarine. Now the American military must make a decision. Should Ramius, a rogue military commander, be destroyed? Is he a threat to America? Jack Ryan puts into action a plan to prove that Ramius is attempting to escape to America, while bringing a tremendous prize—a new type of submarine with a revolutionary propulsion system.

Again, this ties Ramius's action to what's being acted out in the story, a battle between freedom and oppression.

To conclude:

> *In a climactic confrontation, Jack Ryan boards the* Red October *and is able to kill the KGB trained assassin. Working together, Jack Ryan and Ramius stage a fake explosion and sinking of the* Red October. *Through his own undeniable courage and with the aid of Jack Ryan and other Americans, Ramius gains his freedom.*

The Hunt for Red October is a dramatic, compelling story about how the values of freedom defeat oppression.

The spine ends with a reiteration of what was at stake in the story and its fulfillment.

At each step of creating this story spine, it has been clear what's at stake in this story. To simply describe the actions of a story's characters and its plot is to leave out what actually engages the interest of an audience.

You can use a one page story spine to write a synopsis for your script that communicates what is dynamic and engaging about your story. In working with students, I've found they often create a flat first sentence when they talk about a story and its premise in a concrete way. Often, the second sentence of their synopsis was the natural opening. For example, I recently read the first sentence of a synopsis that began:

The Price is a tale of political intrigue and one man's struggle to find redemption in a corrupt world.

The second sentence of the synopsis read, "In a world where advances in science allow a handful of people to create truth for a price, one man struggles with the worth of his soul."

This second sentence is a potential opening sentence for this synopsis. It sets out the issue at the heart of this story while suggesting its plot.

Another possible opening sentence is, "Craig Bowman thought he knew the price of his soul until his was sold."

Choose the opening sentence for your synopsis that communicates the purpose of your story in the strongest, most engaging language. Show your synopsis to others with different opening sentences to find out which version creates the most interest.

A few suggestions:

Your story synopsis should be clear and easy to read. A synopsis that is difficult to read suggests a story that will be difficult to follow. *Keep it simple.*

In your synopsis, move from an overview of your story and plot to a strong, personal sense of the roles of your main characters in acting out your story. Use your description of your main characters and their actions to create a spine for the body of the synopsis.

The more characters you introduce, the more you need to explain, the greater the chance your audience will feel lost. Follow the spine.

Use your synopsis to demonstrate how your plot increases the dramatic tension for your story's main characters. Express the main thrust of the story along your story line and plot line.

Suggest the fulfillment of your story as it is acted out by your plot. For example, the beginning to a synopsis of *Cold Mountain*[35], by Charles Frazier, could read: A wounded Confederate soldier at the end of the Civil War believes that the violence of the war has destroyed his soul, and by making his way home to Cold Mountain, he will find an Indian ritual that will potentially reunite his soul, mind, and body.

This opening naturally suggests the role of the main character in the story, what's at stake, the time, the place, the setting, the goal of the main character, and a sense of why this story would engage the interest of an audience.

The appearance of your synopsis is important. Does your synopsis easily fit onto one page using a 12-point font, with at least one-inch margins and white space at the top and bottom of the page? Remember, a synopsis is a summary of your story, not an explanation of your plot or a history of your characters. If you're asked for those details, of course provide them.

When you finish reading your synopsis, do you feel enthused again about your story, or are you tired of wading through details?

If you're struggling to write a one page synopsis, try starting again. Write about one thing—how your main character feels compelled to act out the promise of your story, and what they go through to fulfill that promise. Mention only those characters who interact with your main character, and the significant events your main character deals with, and the narrative tension your character resolves.

Before you send out your synopsis, set it aside for a few days, then read the synopsis again. Does reading your synopsis make you want to read your story? If not, consider writing another synopsis.

If you are going to offer a verbal synopsis to an agent, editor, or producer, practice it out loud until you're comfortable with what you want to say and you can speak about your story with some of the passion and interest that led you to create it.

Remember, a synopsis is an overview of your story, characters, and plot, not an explanation of your story, characters and plot.

Good luck. Writing a great synopsis can be difficult. Writing a one page story spine can help you create that synopsis.

Chapter Questions

Are you beginning your story synopsis with a dramatically interesting sentence that sets out the role of your main character in acting out your story, and a suggestion of what's at stake for that character?

As you use the story spine to write a synopsis, are you referring the events you describe to your story's promise in a way that creates a clearly identifiable spine for your story?

Does your synopsis read well? Is it fresh, engaging, dynamic? One page?

Does your synopsis clearly suggest what's at stake in your story and build dramatically from beginning to end?

Common Mistakes of Story Structure

When I review manuscripts I often come across similar problems. Different stories, the same structural problems. This chapter sets out what some of those problems are, and some solutions to correct them.

The Basic Mistakes

The basic mistakes most often made in story structure are:

A story's promise isn't suggested in a story's opening scenes.

What's at stake over the story's outcome isn't suggested early in the story.

What's at stake isn't set up as a story question.

The dramatic truths of a story's characters are introduced too deep into a story.

Dialogue is used in a story's opening scenes to make statements about a story's characters, its issues and events instead of setting up questions about the outcome of the story, its events and character issues.

Details of a story don't ring true because characters don't embody dramatic truths.

New characters, events, and issues are presented to make a writer's statements about a story seem fresh, engaging, and dramatic, and to create the impression that the story is going somewhere.

Character issues and goals are presented in a way that they fail to develop drama around their outcome.

Writers introduce more story lines to sustain the waning interest of audiences unclear about what's at stake in their stories.

What's at stake in a story is revealed well into the story, after most people have given up caring.

Because characters don't act to resolve any identifiable dramatic truth, their actions appear to lack purpose.

Writers switch point of view to make a story's action and characters seem fresh.

This is not a complete list of story problems, just a list of the most prominent. What follows are ideas about how to solve some of these problems.

What's at Stake in Your Story?

It's vital that you communicate early in your script that something at stake in the story is in need of resolution. Without this, a story's audience has no sense of the *why* of the story. *Why* they should be interested in it. *What* it's about. *Why* the story's characters are acting in a particular way. *What* the events of the story mean. *That* there will be some kind of dramatic reward if a reader/viewer invests the time to continue with the story.

Writers who struggle almost invariably fail to set up what's at stake in their opening scenes. To set up what's at stake, the storyteller must first perceive that it is a separate issue from introducing characters or setting up a plot. For example: What's at stake in *A Christmas Carol* is whether Scrooge can be renewed. What's at stake in *Pride and Prejudice* is whether Elizabeth Bennet and Mr. Darcy can overcome the traits threatening to keep them apart.

A story that doesn't set up something in need of resolution appears to be a series of events that happen with no particular consequence and that involve characters whose goals are not connected to any discernible purpose. While characters often manifest what's at stake in a story through the issues that they desire to resolve, those issues must be interwoven with the story's core, dramatic issue. Then, as characters act, their actions *advance* the story. For example, because Rocky desires to prove he is somebody and then acts to achieve that goal by fighting Apollo Creed, his actions advance that story. By remaining on his feet when the fight with Apollo ends, Rocky proves the premise of the story.

Why You Must Create a Story Question

Struggling writers often introduce what's at stake in their story as a statement. A statement about a story's issues or the goals of its characters does not set up those issues as needing resolution. It simply comments upon them.

For example, a writer might make a statement that Rocky lacks self-confidence, that Scrooge is a mean and embittered old man, that Mr. Darcy is a very proud young man, that life is difficult, or that crime is wrong.

Many struggling novelists take up to forty pages to make statements about their characters. The storyteller starts with what's at stake and re-creates it as a *story question:* Can Rocky prove he is somebody? Is there anything that can renew Scrooge? Can Mr. Darcy and Elizabeth Bennet overcome their pride and prejudice and find true love? A crime has happened. Can it be undone, avenged, resolved?

When you set up what's at stake in your story as a *story question*, an audience keeps reading to find out the answer to that question. If an engaging character manifests through his or her goals what's at stake in your story, your audience will want to see how those goals are resolved.

To avoid failing to *name* your story, ask yourself: Are your characters making statements about their issues? Are your characters setting up goals and issues as scene questions, or questions to be resolved during the course of the story? This is not to suggest that every scene, chapter, or event begin with a literal question, such as having a character ask Rocky if he wants to gain self-respect. It is important that the writer be clear about the difference between making a statement about a character or story event and setting it up as a dramatic issue that suggests a need for resolution.

The "Why" of Dramatically Weak Dialogue

Writers determined to use the openings of stories to make statements invariably use characters to voice them. Such dialogue is dramatically flat because it has no purpose other then to prove the statements the writer is making. In such stories, dialogue is used to prove that Rocky really does feel like a nobody, that Mr. Darcy really is prideful, that Scrooge really is mean and bitter. Because none of that kind of dialogue dramatically acts out the issues at stake in the story, it's a lecture. Worse still, it's offered with the pretense that it's meant to create a dramatic movement toward resolution. The story's audience feels lied to by such dialogue, or abused and put upon.

Writing Fiction that Rings True

By finding ways to express truths about the human condition through the details of a story, storytellers create stories that speak to audiences. For example, *Prince of Tides* opens with the sentence, "My wound is geography." This sentence speaks to the truth of the story being about healing. By starting with a wounded character, the storyteller takes the audience on a dramatic journey of what this character must do to find healing. Because the details of this story offer a potent experience of his journey toward healing, an audience is drawn in to experience this story's truth through these details. Details not rooted in the dramatic truths that a story explores risk quickly accumulating into an impassable swamp of shapeless details.

If At First You Don't Succeed…

Writers who open stories by making statements about characters often sense something isn't working. Their friends, for example, aren't as excited about their stories as they would like. Editors reject their stories without comment. To overcome this sense of something not engaging the interest of audiences, inexperienced storytellers often introduce more and more dramatic characters and new and more exciting story ideas. These efforts, paradoxically, further weaken their stories. While there's an initial boost in interest around introducing something or someone new, it soon fades.

Similarly, boosting the *volume* of one's statements does not make them more dramatic. For example, to say that Scrooge is not only mean and embittered, he's the most mean, embittered man *ever*, does not make the statement more dramatic. To say that Mr. Darcy is so prideful that he doesn't *deserve* to be in a relationship with a woman might be true, but it doesn't suggest a dramatic consequence to the statement.

To ask, "Can Rocky overcome his doubts about deserving respect?" suggests drama. To say, "Rocky doesn't respect himself," does not.

A variation on boosting the volume of statements is to introduce not just one embittered old man, but two or three.

Another variation on boosting the volume of statements is to write in a way that suggests that if the first story introduced is not interesting enough, then two separate stories with independent story lines and plot lines, or three, are better. The introduction of new characters, issues, ideas, and plot threads creates a momentary sense of interest, but it doesn't last. It doesn't clearly establish a story question based on what's at stake. Worse, it confuses whatever sense of dramatic purpose the writer has created with the introduction of the original story. Confused readers set aside manuscripts. Confused movie-goers tell their friends not to waste their time.

How to Avoid Creating a Lack of Drama in Your Story

The writer of a well-told story arranges the story's elements to create drama. Once what's at stake is set up as a story question, the events of the story dramatically resolve and fulfill that question. Struggling writers often set up characters to have issues, which are then raised as scene, character, or event questions, but which are later resolved in a non-dramatic way.

In a version of *Romeo and Juliet* with flawed drama, Romeo would desire Juliet and have her without too much effort. That is not a story about great love because there's no dramatic effort on his part to attain her. Another example of flawed drama would be if no one blocked Romeo's attempts to attain her. Such a version would offers no reason for anyone wanting an experience about great love to internalize that version of the story.

In a non-dramatic version of *A Christmas Carol*, Scrooge is introduced as a mean, embittered old man. Next scene, Tiny Tim calls him on his ways. Third scene, Scrooge concedes he needs to change. Final scene, he's a new man. That resolves what's at stake, but fails to generate a sustained quality of drama that moves the audience to feel the deeper issue of the story, Scrooge's redemption. We're simply told Scrooge is redeemed; we haven't been led to feel that transformation in Scrooge or within ourselves.

This is not to suggest that a story has only one question that revolves around one issue. Or that all stories revolve around evoking feeling in an audience. It's meant to suggest the series of questions arising from a story's premise all have a common root and that the resolution created fulfills the story's promise. This means that issues, story events, and character goals not related to what's at stake in the story have no influence on the story's outcome. Because they have no effect on the story, they are dramatically inert.

Writers who struggle to create drama often reveal what's at stake about two-thirds of the way into their story. For a screenplay, this means about page ninety.

The problem with this approach is that in order to develop drama around a story's main dramatic issue of human need, the audience needs to know what that issue is. For example, we don't wait until page 90 to find out Rocky wants to prove he's somebody. If we had to wait that long to find out *why* Rocky is fighting Apollo Creed, the story would struggle to develop drama. Similarly, we don't find out on page two hundred that Mr. Darcy's pride and Elizabeth Bennet's prejudice threatens to keep them apart. We find that out in the opening scenes of the story.

In a well-told story, the storyteller generates revelations around what must happen to *resolve* what's at stake in the story. Or, the storyteller creates a revelation around something like the true depth of how what's at stake has profoundly affected a story's characters.

Characters and What's at Stake in Your Story

To have meaning in a story, a character's actions must revolve around a clearly established dramatic purpose. This means that:

> The actions of a story's characters must be arranged to create drama over the course and the outcome of the story itself.
>
> The actions of the story's characters must resolve the story's primary issues and questions. The story's audience should feel that the core issue is being resolved.
>
> A story's character often attains a new state of awareness about himself or herself which allows a story's audience to internalize that experience.

If Rocky doesn't gain self-respect, if Scrooge isn't renewed, if Mr. Darcy and Miss Bennet don't get together, these stories have violated their premises. They have faulty structures. They could, of course, all be recast with different premises that suggest different outcomes. Those outcomes could, for example, demonstrate that love is futile, courage a waste of time, renewal impossible.

It's part of the craft of storytelling that you choose how best to tell a particular story and to fulfill its dramatic purpose in an engaging way.

Switching Point of View (POV)

Switching the POV from one character to another almost always sparks a momentary sense of freshness. Unfortunately, it doesn't last. And switching the POV too often confuses a story's audience about what a story's really about. Generally, confusion is not an effect a writer wants to create.

Unless the writer has a dramatic reason for switching the POV among various characters, writers should find a POV that tells their story and stick with it.

The Was Problem

The verb 'was' lends itself to describing emotions and actions in a passive way (not to be confused with passive voice). 'John was angry' doesn't have the same active quality as 'John clenched his fists.' Try and use verbs that suggest immediate action that has consquences, and avoid overusing 'was' as a default verb of choice. Beginning a story or scene 'It was' or 'There was' compounds the 'was' problem by mating 'was' with a weak pronoun that lacks a context to suggest a meaning. Such openings can work, but they should be examined to see if a stronger alternative is possible.

The Problem with Resolution

Struggling writers often write stories around characters with problems they seek to resolve. The characters then quickly go through the steps of resolving them. That kind of writing can offer a resolution no more dramatic than the fact that two plus two equals four. It may be true, but so what?

To make the resolution of two plus two equals four dramatic, and thus fulfilling, consider the following scenarios.

In the first, you must prove two plus two equals four to someone with no comprehension of math. If you fail, you will die. Is this dramatic? To you, yes. To members of an audience who don't know you, or don't recognize any dramatic purpose to your death, probably not.

In the second scenario, you again must prove two plus two equals four to someone with no comprehension of math. If you fail, everyone in your family will die, or, everyone in your city will die, or the planet Earth will be destroyed.

Does this resolution have a dramatic weight? Yes, more than the first scenario. That is, if people buy into the *idea* and *logic* of the story, they might be curious to know its outcome. If they aren't curious about its outcome, your audience isn't engaged.

In a third scenario, you must prove two plus two equals four to someone with no comprehension of math. This time if you fail, it will prove that true love has no value in our world, that courage has no meaning, that there can be no understanding that leads to a deeper appreciation of life. Does this resolution now have a dramatic weight that an audience feels engaged over its outcome? Yes.

Now, replace the simple numbers in that equation with characters your audience has been led to care about. For example:

Rocky's ability to fight Apollo Creed means that courage in the face of insurmountable obstacles can lead to self-respect.

Scrooge's discovery of his humanity means that there is the possibility that others can find renewal and rebirth.

Dorothy's discovery that it is by facing her issues and fears that she can move forward in life

A successful story *always* offers its audience more than a simple resolution of events. A story offers a *dramatic* affirmation of human needs that are acted out to resolution and fulfillment. Even when that resolution and fulfillment are dark, the journey can still be vivid, potent and illuminating. Spider[36], a dark film by David Cronenburg, promises to take an audience into the life and mind of a broken old man just released from an insane asylum.

While there are many ways a story can lose its way, avoiding these common mistakes will help writers create stronger, more compelling stories.

Chapter Questions

What common mistakes of story structure have you made?

How would you correct some of those problems?

Are you using the opening scenes of your story to make statements about who your characters are?

Do your characters embody clearly defined dramatic truths?

Are you exploring the dramatic truths of your story and characeres through the details you offer?

SECTION FOUR

GETTING STARTED

Getting Started

This chapter offers steps you can follow to get started on your story. Its purpose is to help you cut through the thicket of potential story ideas, characters and plots in your mind to help you focus on the process of turning those ideas, characters, and plots into a particular story.

To begin, let's say you've had an idea for a story. It might be about a character or an event or an issue like courage or overcoming fear. No matter how you come by your story ideas, I want you to think about your story in terms of its core dramatic issue and its issue of human need. Is that issue courage, anger, overcoming fear, redemption, moving out of the dark toward the light? Look into the heart of your story to find this issue. If you're not sure what it is, that's all right. You can start out with one idea, and by working through it, you can find out if you really had something else in mind.

Once you have a working idea and a sense of its promise to an audience, I suggest you create a premise. It should identify the core dramatic issue of your story and its movement toward a resolution that sets up your story's fulfillment. For example, "Overcoming fear leads to confidence." Don't worry if you realize you have a different premise at the end of your story. Many people write to understand what they are writing.

When you create your premise, ask yourself what's at stake in your story. For example, if it's a story about courage, what could be at stake is whether courage has any value in our world. The drama of that particular story would be the acting out of an issue about courage that engages the interest of an audience. If there's nothing at stake in the acting out of your premise, it's possible that you've created a statement. "Honesty is the best policy," for example. You could act out that statement, but you would risk failing to create a story that emotionally or thoughtfully engages your audience.

Remember, from a premise one can deduce two important story issues:

A story question.

What's at stake in the story.

Keep in mind that the answer to what's at stake in a story revolves around setting up the story question that grows out of your premise. This may or may not suggest that you start with a main or minor character. The reason you must, early in your story, set up both what's at stake and the story question is that these elements orient your audience to your story's dramatic purpose.

Next, think of the relationship of your major characters to your story's premise. You can look at characters in various terms. Your protagonist, your main character, might act to resolve what's at stake in your story. Your story's antagonist might serve the function of blocking the movement of your main character in a way that heightens the drama over your story's outcome. Or, the antagonist might act to achieve goals in a way that compels the story's protagonist to react.

Now consider whether your main character and the character who opposes him or her have opposing dramatic truths. Have you introduced these truths with plot events that force your characters to resolve and fulfill something?

Other characters can serve a variety of roles and purposes, and even embody their own dramatic truths. I suggest you start by looking at the relationship between your story and its main dramatic issue, how that relates to your main characters, how your characters act to advance your story toward resolution and fulfillment. Then, consider how to introduce your story's promise through the actions of your characters in a dramatic, engaging way. Bring in minor characters only when they serve a dramatic purpose.

Next I suggest you create a story line and plot line for your story. In fact, I want to tell you right now that....

The failure to create and understand a story line is the single greatest cause of weak storytelling.

Writers who fail to create a story line along with a plot line create stories that are dramatically inert and fail to engage the interest of an audience. To understand the distinction between a story line and a plot is the basis for understanding how to start telling a story on page one.

Once you've found a beginning for your story, the outline process is designed to guide you through setting in motion the process of thrust counterthrust. When one character's actions elicit a response from another character that dramatically advances your story, this process communicates your ability to transport your audience. I suggest that writers of novels use an outline to set out the dramatic purpose of every chapter, then to set out how each chapter serves to advance a story along its combined story and plot lines. By "setting out" I mean *write it down!* If the dramatic purpose of a novel's chapter isn't clear to you, chances are it won't be clear to your readers.

For screenwriters, I suggest you break down the elements of a story into its major events. As you outline the events of the story, you should begin to see the story's overall sense of thrust and counterthrust.

I suggest that playwrights set out their play according to its scenes and acts.

The acid test for the inexperienced writer is this—can you determine if every character issue, event, line of dialogue, and scene description serves to dramatically advance the story? A story without this quality is inert.

When you have a clear sense of the dramatic purpose of your scenes, you have a guide to what kinds of words to use:

Those that best describe the acting out of the dramatic moments of each scene.

I know from working with writers that working through these many story issues the first time can be a mundane, difficult task. The end result, however, is an ability to write stories with a new insight and understanding.

Do you feel ready now to tackle outlining your story so you can get started creating your opening scene? That is the goal of this book.

Chapter Questions

Can you write a first sentence for your story that introduces your main character, suggests a dramatic truth for that character, and raises a question that will draw your audience forward to read a second sentence?

Can you follow that with a second sentence that answers a question raised in the first sentence, while raising a dramatic question that will be answered in a third sentence?

Can you keep going and write enough dramatic, lively, engaging, interesting sentences to complete your novel, screenplay, or play?

Writing Without a Premise

What do you do if you want to start a story without an outline or premise? If you simply want to push the pedal to the metal and see what happens.

To demonstrate this process, I'll use a screenplay I wrote after I saw *The Full Monty*[36], by Simon Beaufoy, and loved its wry humor and its story about empowerment.

I decided I wanted to start with the same issue of empowerment. Wanting to introduce my main character in a playful way, I began my story with Nick Leopard, an Earth-Marshal, in chains before an aged alien. Within a quarter page, Nick is in a raging sword fight with a renegade alien named Bulghar. The fight spills outside a tent and to a precipice where the men wrestle in a death-match.

Then a voice says, "Nick, I have to talk to you." It's Nick's agent who has an urgent message about an A-list producer and a potential job for him. It is then revealed that Nick is in the middle of filming a B-movie (low budget) action film. Nick ignores his agent to finish the scene, even though Bulghar is more interested to hear the news about the producer than in fighting Nick. The scene ends with a victorious Nick dispatching Bulghar. He then learns that Jack, an aged camera operator, got the necessary shot; Nick won't have to use a credit card to reshoot the scene.

Nick's agent excitedly tells him that Sal St. John, a movie producer, is considering Nick for a role in an A-List action film. But Sal wants to meet Nick for a private—very private—audition. For a reason he won't spell out, Nick is worried about this meeting.

His agent tells him to go to dinner with the producer as an Earth Marshal (an action character who fights for justice in Nick's science fiction films) and show some bare chest.

Nick goes to the dinner with Sal St. John, but the intimate dinner turns out to be a formal affair involving Sal's one hundred closest associates. Attending a formal dinner in his Earth-Marshal leather suit, Nick feels foolish. He tries to slip away, but Sal corners him and wants to know why he's unhappy, asking what it will take for him to be happy. It's clear she's attracted to Nick. Nick whispers something in her ear.

To feel he belongs with Sal, Nick needs to rescue her. So Sal sets Nick up in a staged sword fight with Errol, a veteran movie villain. In a rousing sword fight, Nick rescues Sal and captivates the audience of movie industry heavyweights. It appears an A-List action star is born.

But later that evening at Sal's mansion, the shadowy figure of Nick hurries down the stairs. It becomes clear why Nick feared this audition. He's impotent, and he hoped it would never become an issue with Sal. In a cruel twist of fate, Nick's departure from Sal's mansion over a back wall is caught by a photographer, and the reason for his untimely departure hits the news. In a big way. Nick's "problem" now threatens his B-List, action-movie career, not just his shot at being an A-List action star. To make matters worse, Nick realizes his next-door neighbor has been stalking him and secretly watching him from a tree outside his apartment. Developing the idea, I have Nick spend some time "up the tree" behind his apartment, a play on the idea that one tells a story by putting a main character up a tree, then throwing rocks at him or her.

Nick's agent sets him up to see a doctor who prescribes Viagra-like pills, while also setting up a very public date with a starlet. But Nick takes the pill too early, and ends up with a very public erection, which again hits the news. Making matters worse, he takes too many pills later in the evening and has a very comic, very un-sexual reaction. Of course, that gets in the news as well.

At this point, Nick is losing his career. The actor who played Bulghar from the first scene sees a chance to take Nick's place. To make an impression, he rents a lion to take to an audition for Sal St. John. But because he's a C-list actor, he can only rent a thread-bare, testicle-less, male lion.

I didn't start the story with any idea this lion would be making an appearance, but I developed the lion to have a place in the story around this issue of people—and animals—feeling a lack of empowerment. I simply extended the idea to the lion. While writing the story, I wove scenes around the idea of empowerment. For example, it turns out that Nick's neighbor has been stalking him because she has her own issue of empowerment to resolve. Because of breast cancer, she feels she's not a "real" woman, but when she's near Nick, she feels like a woman again. Even though I didn't always know where I was going as I wrote the script, I wrote each scene around some issue of empowerment. It served as a kind of compass as I wrote the story. Knowing and understanding the foundation of my story freed me to concentrate on bringing my story and its characters to life, not writing to "find" them.

As the story continues, each character—including Sal St. John—has to deal with this issue of empowerment, of not feeling strong and capable, of having value to oneself. In the end, Nick manages to save his career and prove his manhood, but not in a way he could foresee when the story began. And the last scene of the movie? The thread-bare, C-List lion does something so dynamic, he's promoted to A-List movie status, an ending that naturally came out of the idea of empowerment.

Then Viagra came out, and I put the script away and moved on, because it made Nick's problem easy to solve.

For storytellers who simply enjoy writing to see where they end up, understanding the process of introducing characters, story ideas, and events around a core dramatic issue, can help to create a strong foundation for your story. This is true even if you decide to use that foundation to build an entirely different house from what you had in mind when you started.

In the end, whatever process you use that helps you create well-told stories is good.

Chapter Questions

If you were to start a story without an outline, what story idea would you choose to be your compass?

What dramatic truth would you give your main character to resolve and fulfill?

How would you introduce that story idea in your opening scenes?

How would you sustain that idea during the course of your story?

From Idea to First Sentence

I know from working with writers that I can help them understand the promise of their stories and the creation of a premise. I can help writers outline their stories. I can help them create a plot and dynamic characters to act out their plot. But often they come back to me with the question: What's the first sentence of my story, and how do I decide that?

This chapter shows how to go from an idea to a premise to a story line and plot line to the first sentence of a novel, play, or screenplay.

Example #1

To show this process in action, let's start with courage as a dramatic issue. Courage is an issue that often appears in stories in some form because characters must have the courage to act if they are to shape a story's course and outcome. Characters who clearly lack the courage to act when confronted with obstacles appear to be automatons shifted around by the story's author.

A premise built around the issue of courage could be:

> *The courage to overcome fear leads to self-confidence.*

This is a simple, straightforward premise. It sets out a story's core dramatic issue: *courage.* It sets out its movement: *overcoming fear.* It sets out the fulfillment set up by the story's resolution: *a character gaining self confidence.*

A simple story line for this premise would read:

> *The introduction of overcoming fear as a dramatic issue. The complications around whether courage can overcome fear. Courage overcoming fear in a way that sets up a new sense of self-confidence for the character who'd been living in fear.*

There is a beginning, middle, and end.

Every story, no matter how convoluted, artistic, surrealistic, action-oriented, or whimsical has a beginning, middle, and end. A key issue that arises out of recognizing a story idea, crafting it into a premise, and creating a simple story line for that premise, is for the writer to see what constitutes the dramatic *beginning* of his or her story, and how to write that engaging opening. One must find a way to *begin* a story through the introduction of its elements, but the story itself, that issue of human need a story explores, exists at a deeper level. For example, a story's audience might not be aware of why people have such a need for stories that express courage, but a storyteller creating a story about courage needs to understand how to bring that issue to life for an audience.

A simple plot line for the above premise would read:

The events that set out overcoming fear as a dramatic issue. The events that show courage and fear in conflict. The events that demonstrate courage overcoming fear in a way that a character gains self-confidence.

A plot in a story also has a beginning, middle, and end. Because the events set out in the plot line interweave with the story line, the events operate to dramatically advance the story.

This is not a call for a simplistic opening that begins:

This is a story about…

Nor does it imply that there's a standard way to begin a well-told story. There is no one way to start a novel, screenplay, or play. Even one written by two different writers from the same premise could be expected to have completely different moods, events, characters. Every writer brings a unique voice to how he or she tells his or her story.

One way to discover and explore opening sentences is to consider sentences on that scale of zero to ten, using zero for obscure, five for obvious, ten suggestive. I encourage writers looking for an opening to be obvious about a character's dramatic truth and situation as a story opens. For example, an obvious possible first sentence for a novel that sets out overcoming fear as a dramatic issue could be:

The shadow passing over Jessica woke her with an uncontrollable feeling of terror.

This first sentence quickly communicates that this is a story about fear. It raises the issue of fear as a question. Can Jessica overcome this fear?

If the audience wants to know more about Jessica and what she's afraid of, it has to read the *second sentence*. I call this a *prime directive* for writing....

If the first sentence or scene of your story doesn't offer your audience a reason to continue, it doesn't matter how wonderful the plot effects or character revelations you reveal on page ninety.

The sentence above about Jessica is designed to be simple and direct, a five on the scale. To write:

Jessica slept in a large bed.

...is to be obscure, a zero on the scale. It simply is an account of what Jessica is doing.

A suggestive sentence about Jessica and the issue of fear could be,

For Jessica night fell twice that Sunday.

In my years of analyzing stories, I've found that the greater the ability of the storyteller, the more directly and potently he or she introduces his or her stories in a way that is quite open about what his or her story is about. He or she then works to create suspense and drama over the course and outcome of his or her story in a way consistent with his or her style of writing and voice.

Another point to note is that these first sentences are not *statements*. They are not written to communicate the level of light in this dark room, the color of the paint on the walls, Jessica's age. They are meant to communicate that this is a story with a dramatic issue at stake.

One could use this story idea about courage and follow the same process to create the first scene of a screenplay wherein we see...

Jessiica sleeps peacefully until a shadow passing over her bed wakes her in terror.

Scene questions that arise are: what's the shadow? Where does her fear come from? Can Jessica overcome her fear?

The story question remains: can she overcome her fear?

If this were the opening scene for a play, we might see…

Jessica is startled awake by a shadow. In her fear, she speaks aloud in a way that sets fear up as a dramatic issue for the story.

Again, set something in motion from the first sentence of your story. However, if it's your intent to introduce your story's world by offering interesting or intriguing descriptions of its environment, you can do that too.

Here are two more examples of this process of writing sentences designed to draw an audience deeper into a story's world.

Example #2

Story issue: redemption.

Premise:

Overcoming greed leads to peace of mind.

Story line:

The introduction of a consuming greed. The complications that arise around whether this greed can be satisfied, or whether it will lead to self-destruction. The peace of mind gained when this greed is overcome.

Plot line:

The events that introduce consuming greed in a dramatic way. The complications that ensue when this consuming greed must be curbed before it leads to a character's self-destruction. The fulfillment set up when this consuming greed is overcome and a character finds peace of mind.

By suggesting that if this character can't overcome being consumed by greed he or she risks self destruction, what's at stake is made clear. In place of a character being consumed by greed, one might substitute the people of a community, or a country. The storyteller creates the degree and sense of urgency for what's at stake appropriate to the story he or she wants to tell.

The first sentence for a novel based on the premise and story line above could be:

Jack woke with one thought insistently repeating itself: either he had the option in his name by noon or he'd lose the McKindrick deal.

Plot question:

Will Jack be able to close the deal?

In this case, I've used a first sentence that is obviously designed to set up plot questions—will Jack be able to make this deal happen, and what are the consequences if he can't? Because they are plot questions that arise from the story, the sentence operates to introduce the story itself.

A possible second sentence:

After the events of the previous week, failure was not an option.

Note how this sentence suggests what's at stake in the story: If Jack can't overcome this consuming greed, will he be able to survive?

It also suggests other, significant events have occurred before this moment. And the third sentence could read:

Even though it was only three-thirty a.m., Jack began writing a list of the people he would start calling at six.

Jack is a determined, obsessed man. A character who could sleep peacefully before a major deal like this would not be suitable for this story.

The opening scene in a screenplay based on the above premise depicts Jack waking, consumed with worry about a deal. As soon as he opens his tired eyes, he's making notes to himself.

As the play opens, Jack wakes and, without realizing the time, makes a phone call to someone who becomes irate at being awakened in the middle of the night.

Example #3

Dramatic issue: finding happiness in life.
Premise:

The courage to move ahead in life leads to happiness.

Story's main character:

Someone who is afraid to live life in the here and now.

Simple story line:

The introduction of an inability to move forward. The complications that arise when someone struggling with life must find the courage to move ahead. The resolution that occurs when he or she confronts his or her fears and learns what it means to be happy in life.

First line for a novel:

Robert woke and saw no way across the bed without waking his nightmare.

Story questions that arises from this sentence:

What will Robert have to do to find his own happiness in life? Can he?

As with the other first sentences, this could be recast, shortened, rearranged, made more artistic. A writer who started a novel with such a sentence, however, has a beacon to guide him or her through creating an opening scene faithful to the story's dramatic purpose. It is a beacon to the truth that this story explores.

Many writers fail at writing a dramatic opening scene because they've taken in the myth that a storyteller creates a story by withholding information from an audience. What those struggling storytellers most often inadvertently withhold, however, is the reason an audience reads the story: an invitation to a world of drama, suspense, action, intellectual stimulation, and passion by a story that will magically transport the reader. An invitation to a world where an audience is engaged emotionally or thoughfully from a story's opening lines. Into a world where a story's readers must read to the end of the story because they have become invested in how a story turns out and what will happen to its characters.

Great writers write *to the point* of the dramatic purpose in an active voice. In Melville's opening for Moby Dick, the words clearly make the point that Ishamel is being overwhelmed by his personal obsessions, and he must go to sea to deal with them. To think that assembling characters, events, and story environments and offering details about them sets out a story's dramatic purpose is to think that assembling a pile of lumber, plumbing fixtures, wiring, and roof shingles creates a well-built house. Just as there is logic behind the design of a well-built house—no matter how straight forward, whimsical, practical, magical, or artistic its final look—there is a logic underlying the construction of a story.

In Catherine Ryan Hyde's novel *Funeral For Horses*, almost every sentence is suggestive, lyrical, heartfelt. I recommend this novel for people who'd like to see powerful examples of how to suggest dramatic truths.

When a story's details are written in a way that they evoke the truth of a story and they make dramatically vivid a story's exploration of that truth, such details of plot, character and scene ring true to an audience. Therefore, a first sentence of a novel, the first line of dialogue of a play or screenplay might be playful, artistic, obtuse, energetic, factual. But something in it needs to tell the story's audience that it's an open door, an invitation into a story's dramatic world. Without that invitation, a story becomes a door unopened.

Understanding how to create an enticing, engaging, first sentence, followed by a second and a third, is one of the arts of storytelling.

Chapter Questions & Exercises

Can you write a wonderfully clever, dramatic, engaging first sentence for your story?

Do you understand how this sentence expresses something about the truth of your story? About the promise of your story?

Now write a second sentence that continues to dramatically explore the truth suggested by the first sentence.

Can you keep going until you've finished your novel, screenplay or play?

Writing with a Free Voice

What's been offered in this book is meant to guide writers to a new sense of freedom. A freedom to write the words that best tell their stories. That make their stories vivid and dramatic. Potent and enjoyable. Engaging and enchanting. Illuminating of engaging ideas. That explore deeply felt dramatic truths.

My purpose is not to load writers with a new set of rules to follow and learn, but to help them internalize some of the basic principles of what creates the effect of a well-told story so that when they write they aren't struggling to come up with a plot or with reasons why their characters act, to figure out what kind of events to describe, to understand why their stories are dramatically inert, to find that combination of details that creates a story world that rings true.

The concepts here are meant to guide writers to set their stories into dramatic motion from their opening words. To go beyond formula writing. To freely explore the world of their story and to write about those worlds with a strong, dramatic voice in a way that dramatically recreates them for an audience.

The concepts here are meant to help writers make a distinction between a story and an account of an event, or a journal entry.

What follows are reviews of movies, books and plays that explore stories written with that free voice by master storytellers.

When the day comes I can include reviews of stories by writers who have been helped by this book, I will be pleased.

SECTION FIVE

REVIEWS OF POPULAR STORIES

FILMS: *THE USUAL SUSPECTS*

L.A. STORY

PLAYS: *ROMEO AND JULIET*

'NIGHT, MOTHER

NOVELS: *THE EXORCIST*

CITY OF GLASS

MOVIE REIVEWS, 2ND EDITION:

AFTERLIFE, MEMENTO, THE SWEET

HEREAFTER, THE FIVE SENSES, LAST NIGHT

Premise and Mystery

Review of *The Usual Suspects*

Screenplay written by Christopher McQuarrie. Directed by Bryan Singer. Actors: Stephen Baldwin, Gabriel Bryne, Chazz Palminteri, Kevin Pollak, Pete Postlewaite, Kevin Spacey, Suzy Amis, Benico Del Toro, Giancarlo Esposito, Dan Hedaya, Paul Bartel. Released in 1995. Available for video rental. Script available for purchase.

On the surface, writing a mystery like *The Usual Suspects* appears to be different from creating other types of stories. Below that surface, it has a similar structure. The purpose of this review is to show how *The Usual Suspects* and the mystery at its heart are constructed.

In earlier chapters I suggested a writer start with an idea for a story's premise, create a premise develop characters, then consider ways to create a dramatically suggestive opening. With a story like *The Usual Suspects*, however, the storyteller must generally understand every element of the story so each part works to create a whole that, when finally fully revealed, creates a satisfying revelation.

Therefore, unlike in my other reviews, I'll begin by stating the premise of *The Usual Suspects*. Then I'll show how the story was assembled to fulfill its premise. I do this with the understanding that the writer, Christopher McQuarrie, might have started with an idea for a character in the story, an idea for the story itself, or an idea for its plot, and then worked back to find his premise.

The premise for the story:

A powerful will can bend others to its purpose.

In this story, Verbal appears to be a weak, talkative man among a group of ruthless gangsters and policemen. In actuality he is Keyser Soze, a man of inhuman will and determination. Because the power of will is the issue at the heart of this story, every character in its world has a purpose that binds them to the story's premise. Every character—policemen and gangsters—is shown to have a dominating, powerful personality. For example, when a drug courier and his bodyguards are cornered in an underground garage, they fight to the death. Every character in this story is tough and determined. If these characters weren't tough and determined, they wouldn't feel the pull of what's at stake in the story, acting out the power of their will. Characters who are weak—with the exception of Verbal—would serve no dramatic purpose.

The Usual Suspects opens in *media res*, in the middle of things. A character named Keaton is on a burning ship with several dead men. He lights a cigarette and starts a fire that will set off an explosion and kill him. The fire is extinguished by a man above him who urinates on the line of flame. Note the symbolism, that the powerful can "piss" on those less powerful.

Keyser asks Keaton, "How you doing, Kid?"

Keaton, "I can't feel my legs, Keyser."

Because Keaton can't feel his legs, he can no longer use his body to act out his will.

Another point, since one element in the story is whether Keyser Soze even exists, note how the audience is told up front, "Yes, he does." It's a way to set this up as a revelation for the police, and for the audience when they realize the significance of the remark, but they still don't know Keyser by sight. That's another revelation. How he masks his existence revolves around his use of his powerful will, which roots his character in the story's premise.

Keyser takes out a gun and two shots ring out. From the dock, a man watches from the shadows as the ship blows up in flames.

Note, in passing, the dead have no will. The fire burns them; they don't react. A minor point, but even dead bodies in this story serve a dramatic purpose.

At this point, the story's plot is about what exactly has happened on this ship, and who Keyser is. These questions are set up to pull the audience into the story and hold its attention. The opening scene advances the story along its plot line because these plot events are interwoven around the story's core dramatic issue, the power of will.

Next, we move to an earlier time when Verbal talks to a grand jury about the event—a truck being hijacked—that led to what happened on the ship. The truck hijacking sets up the reason for why the five suspects are brought in for interrogation. All the suspects are unusually tough willed. Even Edi, the girlfriend of Keaton, is strong willed.

While these men are being rounded up by the police, we're introduced to Kuyon, a detective. He picks up Keaton who is trying to negotiate a legitimate deal involving a restaurant. We then see Keaton, Verbal, and the others in the police lineup. The scene is played with a humorous tone, but again note how *tough* these men are. They are not cowed by the police.

After the lineup, McManus, one of the suspects, comes across as the toughest of the group. The others in the line up are Todd Hockney, Fenster, and Keaton. Verbal sits to one side. It is revealed that Keaton has "hung up his spurs," gone straight. He's become a "lawyer's wife," as McManus says, throwing it in Keaton's face. Keaton doesn't rise to the bait. He's too tough to be baited. He's also aware that somehow the lineup is a setup, that it shouldn't have happened. McManus suggests they do a job, but Keaton wants nothing to do with it. Verbal's voice-over, "This was how it started."

Verbal again talks to us about these men: "They would never break. They would never bend down for anybody." This statement speaks to the story's core dramatic issue about the power of will.

The scene cuts back to the ship in San Pedro, the present. It turns out there were two survivors, and one person is known to be missing. As the scene cuts away, we see a charred body in the harbor.

Kuyon, who picked up Keaton in New York, arrives in Los Angeles. We find out Verbal was a survivor of what happened on the ship, along with a badly burned man. This answers one question: Verbal was the man on the dock who witnessed the explosion. The police suspect the killings on the ship revolved around a drug deal gone bad, a deal worth ninety-one million dollars.

Jeff, a detective, tells Kuyon that Verbal has full immunity and that Kuyon can't touch him. Kuyon insists—uses his will—to make sure he's allowed to interrogate Verbal. Jeff insists that even the Prince of Darkness is protecting Verbal—a reference to the devil that will be made several times. This remark is not a "casual" remark. Just like every remark in this tightly written script, it has a dramatic purpose.

Kuyon insists that Verbal knows something that hasn't yet come out. Specifically, Kuyon wants to know if Keaton is dead. Note, again, the audience has been let in on this, but not quite in a way that it is absolutely clear that Keaton is dead. After all, the audience didn't actually *see* his death. So the storyteller arranges the elements of his story to operate on both the audience *and* the story's characters.

Kuyon is given two hours to break Verbal's story. This gives the story a particular time pressure. It's a technique to orient the audience, that something must happen in forty-eight hours, etc.

The scene cuts to a FBI agent interrogating the burnt man in a hospital. He speaks Hungarian. The burnt man says the name Keyser Soze, which captures the attention of the FBI agent. He orders an interpreter brought in.

In the next scene, Verbal is brought to Kuyon. Verbal looks around the room. We learn only later *why* he looks around the room. Just as every line of dialogue in the story serves a dramatic purpose, so too does the visual information and the order in which we receive it.

Kuyon enters the room. Verbal greets him, "Nice to meet you." We're being set up to believe he's a real wimp. Verbal, true to his name, starts spilling out useless information to Kuyon. Kuyon demands to know what happened after the lineup. Verbal asks for some coffee and is refused, but he talks until he gets what he wants. He uses his *will* to bend the two more powerful men to his needs.

Kuyon accuses Keaton of being a corrupt cop and a good thief. Verbal tries to light a cigarette and fails because of his disabilities, which include a lame foot and hand. Kuyon lights Verbal's cigarette, again bending to Verbal's will. Kuyon tells Verbal, "I'm smarter than you," a statement the story will throw back in Kuyon's face a thousand fold in a way that is pleasurable to the audience. That's why the writer has him make the statement: it sets up a contest of wills that it *appears* Verbal will lose.

The storyteller is always looking for a way to orient the audience to the story's larger dramatic purpose, and then he or she sets up dramatic confrontations and exchanges.

Verbal looks at the bottom of a coffee cup. This act doesn't seem to have a dramatic purpose, but like every moment in this story, it does.

Verbal then begins his narration.

After the lineup, Keaton meets Edi in front of the police station. McManus and the others loiter across the street. Keaton had turned down an offer to be part of a job, but standing there with Edi, he realizes he can never go "straight." The system won't allow it. Note how this point is just *suggested*. The dramatic purpose of the scene is to show Keaton coming to this realization, not to show him *acting* on it. That's the purpose of another scene.

Many writers struggle because their scenes don't have clearly identifiable dramatic purposes. Such scenes fail to suggest a quality of dramatic movement toward a destination that engages the interest of an audience. That's not to say a scene can't have a number of different levels, but a badly written scene has no clear dramatic purpose. Such scenes are just a series of events, actions, and exchanges of dialogue that lead to another scene and another series of weak exchanges.

Verbal goes to see Keaton. He tells him the proposed job will only happen if Keaton agrees to be part of it. Keaton refuses. To goad him, Verbal asks, "Is this your place?" (It's Edi's apartment.) Keaton hits Verbal, who whines, "I'll probably shit blood in the morning."

Keaton decides to participate in the plan, but only if there's no killing involved. The plan revolves around robbing a taxi-service operated by rogue New York cops who ferry around drug dealers and smugglers in police cars. Keaton and the others successfully rob a jewel smuggler riding in a police car, then set the police car on fire. The press, tipped off by Keaton, are on the scene before the police. A number of policemen and officials lose their jobs. Keaton has gotten back at the police for ruining his legitimate business deal with Edi.

The gang decides to go to L.A. to hock the jewels and lie low. Keaton wants to tell Edi he's leaving, but Verbal tells him they'll miss their flight. This moment is developed for its drama, with Keaton and Edi almost seeing each other. Again, every moment is played to heighten its dramatic impact. To separate Keaton and Edi, Verbal again uses his will to bend the tough Keaton to his purpose, although on the surface that's not apparent.

Returning to the interrogation room, Kuyon refuses to believe that Keaton loved Edi and wasn't just using her. Again it becomes apparent that Kuyon wants to know whether or not Keaton is really dead.

At the hospital room, the FBI agent learns there were no drugs on the ship, that the deal revolved around buying people. Again, the burnt man claims he's seen the devil—Keyser Soze. An artist is brought in to draw a picture of Keyser Soze based on his description.

Back in the interrogation room, Kuyon tells Verbal how Keaton once faked his death to avoid being arrested for murder. Note how this will tie in with what's really happening in the story. At this point it only seems like a background detail about Keaton. Kuyon thinks Keaton has used Verbal, which upsets Verbal. Verbal finally reveals something about a lawyer who works for Keyser Soze—Kobayashi. Verbal also tells Kuyon he's sure Keaton is dead, which leads into the next segment of his narrated story.

In L.A., Keaton and the others turn over their stolen jewels to a tough character named Redfoot, who offers them another job. Keaton refuses, but later goes along. Redfoot sets up another jewel heist which goes wrong and turns out to be a drug heist. This upsets the gang.

Meanwhile, the FBI agent finds out that the deal on the ship involved the Hungarian mob and Keyser Soze. Kuyon uses this information to finally pressure the name Keyser Soze out of Verbal.

Continuing his narration, Verbal introduces a lawyer, Koboyashi. Koboyashi explains to Keaton and the others who Keyser Soze is. He explains that Keyser arranged the lineup. That Keyser maneuvered Keaton and the others to this time and place because he wants to use their services. Each man is given reasons for why they can't refuse Keyser's offer: not only will they get ninety-one million dollars if they succeed, but Soze can blackmail each of them using the bad jewel heist and Redfoot if they refuse his job offer. Koboyashi tells them Keyser needs some Argentine mobsters eliminated. Keaton asks why he shouldn't just kill Koboyashi. Koboyashi shows Keaton and the others information that could be used to blackmail each of the men, that Hockney *did* hijack the truck mentioned at the beginning of the story.

Back at Verbal's interrogation he says, "The greatest trick of the devil was convincing people he didn't exist." Verbal talks about Keyser Soze's days in Turkey, that "to be in power you didn't need guns or power, just the will to do what the other guy wouldn't." The heart of the story's *premise* is in that statement. In many action stories, the story's premise is revealed by a character. Again, one creates suspense over a story's outcome *not* by withholding what it's about, but by setting out its dramatic purpose in the form of a story question.

In Verbal's narration of the story of Keyser Soze, the Hungarian gang rapes Keyser's wife and kills one of his children in front of him. They mean to bend him to *their* wills. Keyser, however, kills his own family rather than have them used against him. According to Verbal, "He showed those men of will what will really was." This is another statement that speaks to the story's premise. Keyser then hunts down and kills the men who killed his family. He becomes a myth when he disappears.

Kuyon doesn't believe this story. Verbal says, "The only thing that scares me is Keyser Soze." Kuyon pressures Verbal to testify against Keyser, but Verbal believes that Keyser will have him killed and then disappear.

Back at the hospital, the FBI agent and a sketch artist continue drawing a picture of Keyser as he is described by the burnt man.

In the next scene, Fenster, a member of the gang, tries to run but is killed. Keaton vows revenge on Koboyashi, who he thinks is Keyser Soze. Keaton captures Koboyashi, then learns he's meeting and holding Edi. Keaton realizes he's trapped, that he must do what Keyser wants.

Keaton, Hockney, Verbal, and McManus go to the ship, to see how and if they could survive raiding it. Keaton doesn't think it can be raided, but McManus thinks it can. When the gang returns that night for the raid, Keaton tells Verbal to save himself and to tell Edi, "I tried." The gang sets off on the raid to break up the drug deal. Hockney is killed in a way that suggests something, but it's not clear what. Back in the interrogation room, Kuyon asks Verbal why he didn't run, and Verbal answers that he thought Keaton might do the impossible and make the raid successful.

Keaton realizes there are no drugs on the ship. That the gang's been set up. In a cabin, a terrified man fears Keyser Soze is on the ship. He's then shot by Keyser.

McManus drops dead at Keaton's feet saying, "Strange thing." A few moments later a man shoots Keaton. Verbal tells Kuyon he saw Keyser, a man in a suit.

We next see the ship blow up in flames with Verbal looking on. This is the image we saw in the beginning of the film. A police siren is heard.

Back in the interrogation room, it turns out that the fearful man on the ship was a stool pigeon planning to expose Keyser Soze. The Hungarians had come to "buy" the man as part of their plot to expose Keyser and gain revenge. Edi had been brought in by Koboyashi to be the stool pigeon's lawyer. Kuyon insists that Keaton is Keyser Soze, and that Keaton had Edi killed. This is a major revelation. Kuyon believes that Keaton programmed Verbal to do his bidding. "Why me?" Verbal asks. "Because you're weaker than the others," Kuyon replies.

Verbal breaks down. He appears to accept that Keyser was Keaton, that Keyser was a myth created by Keaton. Verbal is now free to go. He tells Kuyon he will not be a rat, he will not inform on others. He leaves the interrogation room.

The picture of Keyser Soze is finished at the hospital. It is faxed to police.

Verbal retrieves his belongings from the police property room, including his lighter. He exits the police station.

Jeff, the detective, talks with Kuyon about the system of organization in his messy office. "You have to stand back to see the system." It is at that moment that Kuyon realizes that Verbal pulled all the details of his "story" from the

132

details in the room, a black woman named Redfoot, the name Koboyashi from the bottom of a coffee cup, etc.

Kuyon runs out and sees a fax of the picture. Verbal is Keyser Soze. This is the story's major revelation.

Verbal walks down the steps of the police station. Voices overlay Verbal's comments during the interrogation. About the power of will: "My guess is you'll never hear from him (Keyser) again."

Kuyon runs out to try and find Verbal who is Keyser. The audience hears Verbal saying, "The greatest trick the devil ever pulled was convincing the world he doesn't exist."

As Verbal walks down the street, his twisted body straightens and he becomes Keyser Soze. He gets into a car driven by "Koboyashi" and is driven away as Kuyon looks for him helplessly. Verbal says, "And like that...(a puff of breath, like blowing out a candle) he was gone."

In hindsight, one can go back and review this movie and see how every line of dialogue spoke to the story's dramatic purpose. Every scene was true to acting out the story's premise as a question: Could a person of great will—Verbal or Keyser—bend others to his will?

The dramatic answer to that story question which arises from the story's premise is yes. Part of this "yes" is borne out when Verbal kills Keaton, a man he appears to care about. Also having Edi killed, just as Keyser killed his family.

Verbal appears weak because that heightens the story's resolution and fulfillment when it's revealed he is Keyser Soze. In hindsight, the script's premise becomes clear. What also becomes clear is how every element of the story was constructed around fulfilling the story's premise in a dramatic way.

To write a story like *The Usual Suspects*, storytellers should *start* with a clear understanding of their premise. I'm not suggesting that the first draft of the script is what appears in the movie, but that that draft began to set out the dramatic truths of the story. Getting to that understanding will help writers work out the elements of their stories to create plots that resolve their stories in a way that heightens the dramatic pleasure of each story's fulfillment. A script that revolves around creating resolution—this happened, so that happened—can fail entirely to create a quality of story-like fulfillment. This failure is deadly because audiences enter a story's world with a desire to be moved, emotionally and thoughtfully, through a story's presentation of an engaging spectacle. Watching or reading a lifeless sequence of events play out is not moving, no more than watching a clock mechanically tick off time. A ticking clock can be made dramatic, of course, but not if the writer thinks that all it takes is creating a clock and setting up a deadline by which "X" must happen within the minute, or boom. That's plot. It's not a story.

In *The Usual Suspects*, the story's ultimate revelation is both the resolution of the story's plot—what happened on the ship—*and* the fulfillment of the story's premise—could a powerful man of will bend all others to see what he wanted them to see? Yes.

Offering someone a story that is all plot is like offering someone who's hungry a beautiful painting of a meal. While a few people might enjoy the painting and find it a substitute for real food, most people want the satisfaction of a meal. A story satisfies an inner hunger just as food satisfies physical hunger. A story that doesn't satisfy the hunger of its audience is a painting of food.

The Usual Suspects is a wonderful story and plot. I applaud and admire its creator, Christopher McQuarrie. He's a master of the art of storytelling.

Chapter Questions

How do you introduce your story in a way that both suggests your story's dramatic purpose and creates a mystery around its outcome?

How do you create a plot revelation at your story's climax that is surprising to your audience?

How does your surprise plot-climax fulfill your story's premise?

Stories and the Transcendent Experience

A Review of *L.A. Story*

Screenplay written by Steve Martin. Directed by Mick Jackson. Starring: Steve Martin, Victoria Tennant, Richard E. Grant, Marilu Henner, Sarah Jessica Parker, Kevin Pollak, Sam McMurray, Patrick Stewart, Iman. Available in video stores for rental. The script can be purchased. Released in 1991.

A well-told story offers those who enter its world experiences of fulfillment around dramatic issues: Love, the human desire to matter, courage, wisdom, renewal, redemption.

Because of their ability to offer fulfillment, stories can also take readers beyond an internal experience to a state of transcendence. I define a transcendent experience as one in which we feel and experience knowledge or feelings about life above and beyond our normal state of feelings or thoughts.

We desire these transcendent experiences because life is often fragmented. Issues are unresolved. Feelings are unexplored or unexplained; perhaps they are too painful to explore. Events aren't conclusive. Mysteries aren't resolved.

How does one create a story that offers this experience of transcendence? To demonstrate how this is achieved, I'll break down the structure of *L.A. Story*.

L.A. Story opens with a hot dog flying through the sky and a silly song being sung in the background. These are cues that this story is going to offer experiences outside normal "reality." The story then introduces a number of sights, many comic, setting out life in L.A.

The audience is next introduced to Harris K. Telemacher, a wacky television weatherman with a degree in the Arts and Humanities. Harris, in his voice-over, quotes Shakespeare, a recurring motif.

On his way to lunch, Harris narrates that life is "sound and fury, signifying nothing." He passes a man on the side of the freeway looking up at a road sign that offers traffic reports.

At lunch, Harris meets Sarah, a newcomer to Los Angeles. During this encounter, the music and tone of every exchange featuring Sarah is serious. The audience is being directed to see Sarah as a serious person, not a projected persona like the others at the lunch.

After lunch, Harris drives off without his girlfriend. Thinking of Sarah, he's already existing outside his normal reality. Later, Driving on the freeway, Harris's car dies near a freeway sign. Harris comments, "There are two events in my life that I consider to be magical… The first is about to happen."

At that moment, the wind blows through the trees in a way that suggests even the "wind" is alive in this story. This is a point Martin explores, how we live in a world that is alive, that interacts with us.

As Harris stands before the freeway sign, it asks, "RUOK," i.e., "Are you okay?" Harris assumes he's being filmed, especially when the sign asks to be hugged. But he obliges and hugs the sign. Harris has connected with the sign. Through his willingness to reach out in spite of his fear of being ridiculed, he makes a deeper connection to life.

The sign tells him, "I see people in trouble and I stop them. L.A. wants to help you." This suggests we are watched over, cared for, in ways we cannot always comprehend. The sign continues, "U will know what to do when you unscramble How Daddy is doing." Harris, puzzled, goes on his way.

The next day, the sun rises faster than normal. This is a special, magical world that operates at its own pace.

The next scene shows Harris and Sarah waking up. Through the magic of editing they "share" their morning, including a shower in the "water of life," even thought they are in different places.

After his shower, Harris is inundated with mail that flies in a stream through his front door. This comic moment has a serious point: he's inundated with contact, but none of it is personal. None is the fulfilling kind he desires, that affirms who he is. Even though this story is a comedy on one level, on another it is very observant of the human condition, of our need to feel we matter.

Harris drives half a block to see his friend Ariel. Again there is a connection to Shakespeare—a character with the name of an "elemental," a creature not of this earth. Elemental Ariel and Harris go to a museum, where Harris does some magical skating. In the museum, Harris is alive and vibrant.

Harris later meets Sarah for an interview. They end up at a graveyard. It's a comic scene that revolves on one level around the finding of the Great Blunderman's skull, a man Harris knew, a "fellow of infinite jest." Again, Harris feels the moment with Sarah; it's not just an ordinary, hectic moment of the kind he generally passes through in his life without much thought or feeling. He finds her realness attractive.

Sarah leaves Harris to go off with her boyfriend, Roland. Harris goes to a clothes store and meets a young girl named SanDe, but doesn't get her phone number. Later, when he drives by the freeway sign, it tells him, "You should have got her number."

Soon after Harris makes a jest about his girlfriend having an affair with his agent, and it turns out to be true. Harris plays the part of a jilted boyfriend, but he's really happy to find himself free from his persona-laden girlfriend.

Harris returns to the freeway sign to ask it if he can get out of the weather business, too. The sign tells him, "I was a bagpipe, but I can't play." From the sound it makes, others would agree. So even the sign has some need. It then tells Harris, "The weather will change your life."

Harris and Sarah have dinner, then she takes him home and is ready to leave when her car starts rolling along the street but going uphill. Then its lights come on, and its doors open. Harris understands the sign is calling them, and he urges Sarah into the car.

The magical spirit of life now manifests in stronger and more direct ways in Harris's life. Note that the wind blows in a way that suggests the magical forces of life will be manifesting very strongly around Harris. Harris takes Sarah and they stand before the sign. While Sarah speaks of logic, the sign tells Harris, "Kiss her, you fool." He kisses her. She continues to speak of the rational reasons this kiss should not be happening. Again the sign tells Harris to act, "Kiss her again." Then it says, "Let your mind go and your body will follow."

Sarah isn't sure she wants to be with Harris. She tells Harris that he simply amuses himself with his antics and that he creates noise to fill the void that is his life.

Harris and Sarah leave the road sign and go to see his mother at a presentation, but they leave the gathering to be alone in a secluded spot to make love. During this scene, the moon is reflected in a pool. Soft music plays. These images suggest the intimacy of life. "Wonderful, wonderful you," Harris narrates about Sarah in his thoughts. The music swells. As they walk together, they become a boy and girl wearing adult clothes. They pass some stone lions, and even the lions turn their heads to see the young lovers, to see this expression of human love.

We are led to experience this transcendent moment of love transforming everything it touches. These scenes flood our senses with images about love, and they show us how it can be pure and deeply felt.

The story creates this transcendent moment by:

1. Flooding our senses with dramatically potent images, man and woman, boy and girl.
2. Swelling music, another way to flood the senses with sounds that are uplifting.
3. Stone lions turning their heads, a visually transcendent image that suggests that in the face of such powerful love, even stone lions will come to life.
4. Harris and Sarah become young and pure, another visually transcendent image.

These quick epiphanies about the nature of love are meant to move an audience both to feel and think about the nature of pure love, to experience that state.

In spite of what they've just shared, Harris and Sarah then make separate plans to go to the beach, but with other partners. Sarah discovers Harris there and finds out he's sleeping with SanDe. What has been presented to be pure turns to ashes and defeat in Harris's mouth. Sarah vows to leave Harris. Harris, through narration, states, "If I could, I would turn the wind around…" He is speaking of that plea that life hear and respond to our needs.

The moon in the cloudy sky suggests pain and darkness.

Harris narrates, "We don't always know the moment love begins, but we always know when love ends." This is a deeply felt emotion spoken by a man starving for affection and intimacy who's blown his chance at just that.

Harris sits alone in his house, deeply feeling the loss of Sarah. Sarah boards a plane to leave L.A. Music swells, cueing us that something important is about to happen.

As the plane rolls down the runway, fog begins to roll in. The lights on the freeway sign blinks on. A flute plays in tones that suggest mournful longing A barometer changes rapidly. Clouds, a storm, music. Harris is deep in concentration.

In the sky, lightning strikes. Harris's thoughts have manifested themselves and gone out into the universe to say, "Don't let Sarah leave!"

The plane cannot take off. The music swells as the plane is forced by Harris and the universe to return to the airport. Both Harris and Sarah raise their hands to their respective windows, and we "know" they are touching hands.

As the hands of Sarah and Harris touch in love, the freeway sign explodes in light. Harris sees the lights of a cab approaching. Sarah gets out and she and Harris kiss. The storm ends.

The storm mirrored Harris's feelings. In this magical world, the world is alive to his feelings and is transformed by them.

Harris, again narrating, says, "A kiss may not be the truth, but it's what we wish were true."

Sarah and Harris again stand before the freeway sign. It asks for a gift of cable television. It wants to feel more connected to our world. Again, the sign expresses that desire to feel connected to the world.

Sarah then figures out an answer to the sign's riddle, "How Daddy is Doing." The answer is simplicity itself.

The sign flashes, "There are more things in heaven and earth."

Yes, and through this kind of story, we allow ourselves to experience how life can flow through us in powerful, unexpected ways; how the forces of life can respond to our thoughts and needs.

The freeway sign plays "Amazing Grace" in a way that swells and is glorious, unlike the sign's earlier, grating attempt to play music. The freeway sign itself has been transformed by Sarah and Harris's love. Lights come on all over L.A. This is a transcendent moment. We are all watched over. Harris narrates, "Romance does exist in the heart of L.A." The moon embraces the lovers as they kiss.

Again note how this final experience is designed to fill our senses, to flood our eyes with the light of beautiful images that move us to feel states of love, to fill our ears with beautiful music, to fill our inner selves with feelings and epiphanies about the power of love.

The story fulfills our need that Harris and Sarah find a way, through the help of the universe, to get together, so we can believe in our own lives such a powerful, pure state of love exists.

Any story that creates a state of intense emotions, thoughts, or illuminations around a desirable issue in a way that suddenly elevates or floods the senses, or that enlivens the inner state of feeling in an intense way, can produce a transcendent experience.

A storyteller desiring to create that experience must be aware of how to arrange the elements of a story. The storyteller must set out story elements in a way that quickly "lights up" the interior world and senses of the audience.

This is why a story, any story, must be of consequence if it's to fully engage the attention of its audience. It must be about something people recognize and desire to feel and experience in a full, rich way.

Understanding how to create a story that helps its audience transcend ordinary lives and feelings is a part of the art of storytelling.

Chapter Questions

How does your story operate to help your audience transcend ordinary feelings?

What stories help you transcend ordinary life?

How do you structure your story to trigger a transcendent experience for your audience?

The Power and Passion of Love & Hate

A Review of *Romeo and Juliet*

Romeo and Juliet was written by William Shakespeare. The edition of the play reviewed was published by The New Folger Library, Washington Square Press, ISBN 0-671-72285-9.

This review explores how Shakespeare structured this story and brought it to life.

Romeo and Juliet opens with a prologue announcing that the story's star-crossed, young lovers will die and their deaths will reconcile their warring clans. Shakespeare opens his story by boldly announcing the climax of its plot. How can he get away with this? Because the better the storyteller, the stronger his understanding that a story is a journey and that every step of that journey must be made engaging and dramatic, must be more than the sum of its parts. Shakespeare does what most inexperienced writers would be loathe to do—give away his ending—because what makes his story satisfying is a separate issue from the mechanics of its plot.

Furthermore, by telling the audience the story's outcome, Shakespeare gives the story an added poignancy. Knowing the lovers will die makes their every step toward that fate more deeply felt. This knowledge that the lovers will die speaks to drama as not only the anticipation of action, but also the anticipation of feelings and thoughts that are aroused in the story's audience.

Act One

SCENE ONE

Act One opens with some of the men of the Capulet clan meeting those of the Montague clan in the street. A brawl erupts, citizens join in, and the heads of the houses of Capulet and Montague come upon the scene. The Prince of the City then arrives. He declares that if there is more fighting, those who are guilty will face death.

The dramatic purpose of this scene is to introduce the two families who are bound together by an ancient blood feud that has grown to a lethal hatred. The scene does this through a measured introduction of characters that gives the audience time to assimilate who a particular character is, the personality of each character, and the relationships between the characters. Because this story is about a conflict between love and hate, introducing the hate that fuels the story's action also serves to set the story into motion.

In the aftermath of the brawl, a question arises as to the whereabouts of Romeo, a young Montague. It is revealed that he has been shedding tears and avoiding his kinsmen, but the reason why is unclear. It is left to Benvolio to discover the cause of Romeo's distress.

Romeo enters as the others exit. Through Benvolio's probing, the audience quickly learns that Romeo is lovesick.

"Out of her favor where I am in love," he laments. (I. 1. 173.)

The dramatic purpose here isn't to withhold that Romeo is lovesick, but to present that he is. Struggling writers often withhold the real feelings of their characters for some later revelation. Shakespeare, on the other hand, introduces Romeo in a state of intense emotion and then finds a way to escalate the intensity of his emotions.

SCENE TWO

The Senior Capulet enters, mentioning the ban on any further fighting and that this ban should be easy to uphold. Note how Capulet's words will come back to haunt him. During this scene, Count Paris reminds Capulet of his desire to wed Juliet, a girl not quite fourteen. Capulet wishes that Juliet be older before she weds, but Paris presses his suit. Capulet invites him to a party that night, and they exit.

Our introduction to Juliet, even while she remains off stage, offers a sense of who she is. Further, we see that Juliet's life is at a moment of potential transition from young girl to wife. She too is a "ripe" character.

Enter Benvolio with Romeo, who is still caught up in being lovesick. They immediately come upon a servant sent out by Capulet to announce a party, but the servant cannot read. He asks Romeo to read the invitation list. It turns out that Rosalind, for whom Romeo pines, has been invited to this party. The servant, grateful to Romeo for reading the list, invites him to the party as long as he's not a Montague.

Benvolio suggests Romeo go, that seeing some of the town's other beauties might aid his recovery from his infatuation with Rosalind. Romeo answers, defending Rosalind, "One fairer than my love? The all-seeing sun / Ne'er saw her march since first the world begun." ((I. 2. 99—100.)

Shakespeare maintains a measured, brisk, pace throughout these opening scenes where he introduces us to the principle characters and their issues. The playwright then begins bringing them together in a way that escalates the story's dramatic tension. Romeo's going to a party at the Capulet's is inherently dangerous.

SCENE 3

This scene opens with Lady Capulet, Juliet's nurse, and Juliet, alone in Juliet's chambers. The nurse is a folksy, humorous character. She ends a long answer to a simple question with the hope she live long enough to see Juliet marry. That becomes the opening for Lady Capulet to broach to Juliet her parents' desire she consider marrying Paris.

Juliet answers, "I'll look to like, if looking liking move. / But no more deep will I endart mine eye / Than your consent gives strength to make it fly." ((I. 3. 103—105.)

They exit to attend the party.

Again the author's measured, brisk pace of introducing characters and their issues to maintain each scene's dramatic impact.

SCENE 4

When Romeo, Mercutio, and Benvolio enter the party, they discover it is a masquerade, which means their faces are not visible. Romeo and Mercutio pause to talk about dreams, then Romeo says, "I fear too early, for my mind misgives, / Some consequence yet hanging in the stars." ((I. 4. 113—114.) Something about this moment troubles him, but he nevertheless goes to the party.

Having Romeo and company pause before entering the party allows the drama about what will happen at the party to build.

SCENE 5

Capulet welcomes Romeo and company to the party. Romeo sees Juliet and exclaims, "O, she doth teach the torches to burn bright!" (I. 5. 51.)

The purpose of this scene is to show Romeo falling in love with Juliet, so it is not delayed. The question now becomes, what will be the outcome of this love he feels for her?

Many writers struggle because they build up to a moment of dramatic tension and then back away. Shakespeare begins a scene with dramatic tension and quickly works to heighten that tension.

Tybalt, who crossed swords with Benvolio in scene one, recognizes Romeo's voice and sends for his sword. The elder Capulet orders Tybalt to stand aside, and even praises Romeo for being known as virtuous. Allowing Romeo to stay is an act that will come back to haunt him. Tybalt protests, but Capulet rebukes him and orders him to not upset the party. Romeo takes Juliet's hand and speaks to her, "If I profane with my unworthiest hand, / This holy shrine, the gentle sin is this: / My lips, two blushing pilgrims, ready stand /To smooth that rough touch with a tender kiss." (I. 5. 104—107.)

It is the purpose of the scene to show how quickly and deeply Romeo falls in love with Juliet. His falling in love is not delayed, nor does it happen off stage.

Juliet is quickly swayed by Romeo's passion. Juliet responds, "Good pilgrim, you do wrong your hands too much, / Which mannerly devotion shows in this; / For saints have hands that pilgrims' hands do touch, / And palm to palm is holy palmers' kiss. ((I. 5. 108—111.) Romeo kisses Juliet once, then again. Juliet's nurse calls her away, and Romeo learns from the nurse that Juliet is of the house of Capulet. Romeo exclaims, "O dear account! My life is my foe's debt." (I. 5. 132.) Again, the playwright maintains his brisk pace of setting up and advancing the story.

Juliet, on learning Romeo's identity, says, "My only love sprung from my only hate! / Too early seen unknown, and known too late! / Prodigious birth it is to me / That I must love a loathed enemy." (I. 5. 151—155.)

This is the end of act one. All the major elements are in place: the hatred of the Montagues and Capulets, the idea that Romeo is lovesick and in love with the idea of love, the fate that will befall the next person to disturb the peace, and finally—the fact that Romeo and Juliet are in love. The curtain closes on a note of high drama and emotion. The storyteller has brought the audience to this height of emotion because very little is withheld for some later plot effect or revelation. What is important to the setting up and advancement of the story has been presented in a clear, dramatic way.

When Shakespeare writes that one character doesn't like another, an audience can surmise the two will meet in either that scene or the next. Because of this arrangement of the story's elements, the audience develops a sense of trust that the playwright won't introduce characters for no clear dramatic purpose, or introduce information but then delay its import.

Shakespeare writes every moment of every scene to bring out its drama. If characters are angry, they speak poetically of their anger and what they intend to do to resolve it. When they are lovesick, they speak of heavy hearts; vengeful, they speak of the joys of vengeance. Each moment he creates heightens the drama of that particular moment. The struggling writer is forever doing what I call describing the furniture. He or she describes characters, events, and environments as if from rote, while the dramatic richness of what should be the heightened moments of a scene are held back for some later revelation or perceived plot effect. Shakespeare is a master of the moment, the scene, the act, the story

Wonderful introductions to characters who can be expected to dramatically advance the story in its second act.

Act Two

SCENE ONE

The second act opens with a Chorus that posits a problem for Romeo and Juliet, "Being held a foe, he may not have access." (II. 1. 9.) However, the Chorus also points out, "But passion lends them power, time means, to meet, / Temp'ring extremities with extreme sweet." (II. Chorus. 13—14.)

Just as the opening lines of the chorus foretold the end of the story in the prologue, this chorus foretells what will soon transpire in the second act. Again, with a master storyteller, it's the journey the story creates for its audience that is moving, not a withholding of the destination for dramatic effect.

The action of the scene opens with Romeo's two lines, "Can I go forward when my heart is here? / Turn back, dull earth, and find thy center out." (II. 1. 1—2.)

Romeo goes over a garden wall into the Capulet estate.

Romeo is a lovesick, rash, impulsive character. Shakespeare reveals that to us by having Romeo voice just two lines before going over the wall to return to Juliet. He doesn't think about it, doesn't discuss it with others, he simply acts on his feelings in a way that advances the story.

Many writers struggle because they spend a great deal of time setting up why characters will do a particular thing when they eventually meet. Shakespeare arranges for characters to meet because it is in those moments that their goals and feelings are naturally revealed.

Walking along a dark road, Benvolio and Mercutio see Romeo go over the wall into a field. Both Benvolio and Mercutio realize there's no point in trying to find Romeo, who they think has gone off to find Rosalind.

SCENE TWO

Romeo goes forward across a field and to the Capulet's estate. Standing in a garden, he sees Juliet on a balcony. He speaks of his love for her, "Oh, that I were a glove upon that hand, / That I might touch that cheek." (II. 2. 25—26.)

Juliet speaks from her heart, "O Romeo, Romeo, wherefore art thou Romeo?" (II. 2. 36.) She continues, "What's in a name? That which we call a rose / By any other name would smell as sweet." (II. 2. 46-47.) Poetic language treasured through the ages. Juliet speaks of her feelings for Romeo, "My love as deep, The more I give to thee, / The more I have, for both are infinite." (II. 2. 141—142.) She adds, "Yet I should kill thee with much cherishing. / Good night, good night. Parting is such sweet sorrow / That I shall say "Good Night" till it be morrow." (II. 2. 198—200.)

Beautiful, beautiful language. Spoken in the moment, from Romeo's heart, offered to Juliet's heart, and passing through the hearts of the audience. With these words Shakespeare is not limiting himself to describing what Romeo and Juliet look like as they speak to each other, but bringing out the full range of emotions the characters express in a situation Shakespeare has created by design for that purpose.

SCENE THREE

Romeo meets with Friar Lawrence and asks that he perform the marriage to Juliet. Friar Lawrence chides Romeo about being so recently lovesick over Rosalind. But he agrees to the marriage because it would end the feud between the two clans. Romeo says of his marriage, "Oh, let us hence. I stand on sudden haste." (II. 3. 100) Friar Lawrence replies, "Wisely and slow. They stumble that run fast," (II. 3. 101.)

The Friar's comment foreshadows what acting in haste will lead to.

Romeo meets Juliet and the Friar arranges their marriage. Again, the story is advancing.

SCENE FOUR

Mercutio and Benvolio wonder about Romeo and think he's still madly in love with Rosalind. It is revealed that Tybalt has sent some kind of challenge to Romeo's father, possibly a challenge to duel Romeo.

The nurse comes upon Mercutio and Benvolio with a message for Romeo from Juliet, but first there is a comic exchange between the nurse and Mercutio. Their exchange varies the pace of the story. Romeo asks the nurse to have Juliet meet him at the cell of Friar Lawrence to be married.

SCENE FIVE

Juliet waits impatiently for the nurse. When the nurse returns, she delays relaying Romeo's message and instead offers a list of her aches and pains. When Juliet does finally learn that all she needs to do to marry Romeo is to meet him at Friar Lawrence's cell, she is ecstatic.

SCENE SIX

Romeo and Juliet meet at the Friar's cell. They leave with the Friar to be married. The Friar encourages "Come, come with me, and we will make short work, / For, by your leaves, you shall not stay alone / Till Holy Church incorporate two in one." (II. 6. 35.)

The preceding four scenes have all been brief and focused, and therefore have quickly advanced the story. Because the story is not about the details of how Romeo and Juliet get married, Shakespeare does not dwell on those scenes. Once a scene has fulfilled its purpose of advancing the story in a dramatic way, it is concluded.

This scene ends Act Two. The act answers the question, can Romeo and Juliet be together? It also raises the question, will they be able to be together in the third act? It's important that a storyteller be able to advance the story in the second act at a measured but brisk pace, even while leaving open a question to draw the audience back into the third act. Many writers struggle because they withhold and delay a great deal of a story to create a single, powerful revelation. Shakespeare, however, made the journey of the story itself a series of potent revelations. And each act ends of a revelation or dramatic note that maintains a hold on the attention of the audience.

Act Three

SCENE ONE

The intensity of the story is heightened in the opening scene of Act Three. Benvolio and Mercutio come upon Tybalt. The three taunt each other, and then Romeo arrives on the scene. Tybalt challenges Romeo to a duel, which Romeo refuses, hinting that he and Tybalt have no cause for quarrel now: "And so, good Capulet, which name I tender / As dearly as mine own, be satisfied." (III. 1. 73—74.)

Romeo's words infuriate Mercutio, who draws his sword and challenges Tybalt. Tybalt mortally wounds Mercutio. Romeo responds, "…Tybalt, that an hour / Hath been my cousin! Oh, sweet Juliet, / Thy beauty hath made me effeminate /And in my temper softened valor's need." (III. 3. 117—120.)

Tybalt again challenges Romeo and is slain. The Prince, together with the heads of the Capulet and Montague clans, is immediately upon the scene. For his part in Tybalt's death, the Prince exiles Romeo from Verona.

That ends the scene.

SCENE TWO

Juliet is awaiting Romeo when the nurse enters with news of his banishment. Juliet speaks of killing herself out of grief at the loss of Romeo, "I'll to my wedding bed / And death, not Romeo, take my maidenhead." (III. 2. 149—150.)

The nurse promises to find a way to bring Romeo to her.

SCENE THREE

Friar Lawrence tells Romeo he is banished, thinking it a good end to a bad situation. Romeo feels only the loss of Juliet. The nurse arrives with the news that Juliet is mourning the banishment of Romeo. Plans are made for Romeo to come to Juliet, and for the Friar to arrange their departure from Verona.

SCENE FOUR

Count Paris approaches Capulet and pressures him to agree to his marriage to Juliet. Capulet gives in and agrees to a marriage that takes place within three days.

The dramatic purpose of this scene is to escalate the pressure on Juliet to forsake Romeo.

Shakespeare introduces characters when they serve a dramatic purpose. For example, he earlier introduced Count Paris asking for the hand of Juliet. That scene served the dramatic purpose of showing Juliet being considered for an arranged marriage. The Count's new proposal escalates the drama around whether she can be with Romeo. Similarly, Friar Lawrence enters the story only when he has a dramatic purpose to serve, arranging the marriage of Romeo and Juliet. He's not introduced earlier as a background character because that would serve no dramatic purpose. Many writers struggle because they use the opening scenes of their plays to introduce characters whose dramatic purpose in the story only becomes clear later.

SCENE FIVE

As another day dawns, Romeo and Juliet prepare to separate. Juliet says, "Then, window, let day in, and let life out." (III. 5. 41.) Romeo responds, "Farewell, farewell, one kiss and I'll descend." (III. 5. 42.)

Juliet has a premonition of Romeo's death, which frightens her. Romeo departs, and Juliet's mother enters the room. She vows to Juliet that when Romeo is exiled, someone will be sent to kill him. When Juliet is told of the plan that she is to marry Count Paris, she counters that it is only Romeo she will wed.

Juliet's father refuses to hear why she resists marrying Count Paris. He exits the stage. Juliet's mother likewise will not listen to Juliet and also exits. Juliet sends word to her parents that she's going to see Friar Lawrence to seek absolution. Her final words are, "If all else fail, myself have power to die." (III. 5. 255.)

In this scene, Juliet shows herself to be a character willing to die rather than submit to her parents concerning the marriage to Count Paris. Hearing these words at the end of Act Three, the audience is made aware of to Juliet's dramatic dilemma and to one solution; it is also drawn to the next act to find the answer to what she'll do. Another powerful, well-developed act.

Act Four

SCENE ONE

Count Paris visits Friar Lawrence to arrange his marriage to Juliet. Paris explains her reluctance as arising from her grief over Tybalt's death. Juliet arrives and speaks to Paris about her love for Romeo, but in a veiled way. He, not understanding, takes his leave. Juliet pours out her anguish to the Friar, and shows him the knife she will use to take her life if something cannot be done. The Friar gives Juliet a potion that will make her appear dead, explaining that she should take it the night before her wedding to Paris. Juliet agrees to take it. Once again she acts out her determination to control her own fate. The Friar also tells Juliet that he will send a note to Romeo via a courier so that Romeo will not be alarmed at her apparent death.

Once again, Shakespeare brings together the principles whose actions advance the story. Because Romeo's thoughts about his exile to another town and his journey there, for example, serve no dramatic purpose to this story, so they are not included.

SCENE TWO

Juliet returns home and finds her father preparing for her wedding. She pretends that she will honor his request to marry Count Paris. Her father is so delighted, he says the wedding should happen the very next day.

Shakespeare deliberately heightens the dramatic pressure not only on Juliet, but on the audience as well, the storyteller is always looking for ways to increase the dramatic pressure on characters, not reduce it.

SCENE THREE

Juliet speaks to her mother, saying that all is in preparation for the next day. These are words rich in irony. Juliet explains, "No, madam, we have culled such necessaries / As are behooveful for our state tomorrow." (IV 3. 7-8.) She takes out the vial and wonders if it is really a poison that will kill her and save the Friar the embarrassment of having married her to Romeo. Juliet drinks from the vial with these words, "Romeo, Romeo, Romeo! Here's drink. I drink to thee." (IV. 3. 59—60.)

SCENE FOUR

The elder Capulet and the nurse stay up preparing for the wedding. When they hear the approach of Count Paris, Capulet sends the nurse to awaken Juliet.

SCENE FIVE

The nurse finds Juliet seemingly dead and calls for others to come see Juliet's body. Lady Capulet is first on the scene, followed by Juliet's father. They mourn Juliet's death. Moments later, Friar Lawrence arrives with Count Paris. Friar Lawrence instructs the parents that Juliet's body be taken to the church for her internment

These five scenes constitute the Fourth Act. They all revolve around Juliet's determination to do whatever must be done to be with Romeo and not marry Count Paris. In these scenes, Juliet comes to life as a fully dimensional character whose actions advance the story to its final act.

Act Five

SCENE ONE

A man brings Romeo news of Juliet's death. Romeo is bereaved, but still asks if the man brings a letter from Friar Lawrence. When the answer is no, Romeo instructs the man to hire a horse to take him to Verona. As soon as the man departs, Romeo speaks of his intentions, "Well, Juliet, I will lie with thee tonight." (V. 1. 36.) As always, Romeo speaks directly about his intentions, and by making his intentions clear, the drama of the story is heightened.

When Romeo tries to buy a poison to take his life, the apothecary hesitates because it's against the law. Even this moment in the story is presented in a way that its drama is heightened. Will the apothecary sell Romeo the potion or not? The answer isn't just given to us that he will. The audience is allowed a moment to *not* want the apothecary to sell Romeo the potion. In that way, the emotions and attention of the audience is held within the story.

SCENE TWO

Friar Lawrence is told the letter he sent to Romeo about Juliet's seeming death was not delivered. Friar Lawrence realizes he must immediately break in to Juliet's tomb to forestall a new tragedy.

SCENE THREE

Paris comes to see Juliet in her tomb. Soon afterwards, Romeo arrives, determined to join Juliet in death. He asks that Balthasar, his companion, take a letter to his father. Paris comes upon Romeo and blames him for Juliet's death, thinking that she killed herself over grief for Tybalt. Romeo tries to tell Paris that he's at Juliet's tomb to join her, but Paris insists on taking Romeo into custody. Romeo, not recognizing in the dark who challenges him, draws his sword and slays Paris, who asks with his dying words to join Juliet. Romeo realizes then that it is Count Paris, a kinsman of Mercutio, and this adds to his grief, that he has taken the life of someone who also loved Juliet.

Romeo opens Juliet's tomb and says, "For here lies Juliet, and her beauty makes / This vault a feasting presence full of light." (V. 3. 85—86.)

Romeo kisses Juliet, then drinks his poison. As soon as he falls dead, Friar Lawrence comes on the scene and finds Paris and Romeo. At that moment, Juliet awakes and asks for Romeo. Friar Lawrence, hearing others approach, wants to take Juliet away to be a nun, but she refuses. Friar Lawrence leaves, and Juliet picks up Romeo's dagger, saying, "O, happy dagger, / This is thy sheath. There rust, and let me die." (V. 3. 175.176.) She kills herself.

Others arrive and a search is mounted to find out if anyone is in the vicinity who understands what has happened. The heads of the Capulet and Montague clans are sent for, as is the Prince of Verona. Balthasar and Friar Lawrence are also found and brought to the tomb. Finally, Romeo's father arrives with news that his wife died that night.

The Prince demands an explanation of the events. Friar Lawrence tells him how events transpired to lead to the deaths of Romeo, Juliet and Paris. The Prince reads Romeo's suicide note, then turns to Capulet and Montague and says: "Where be these enemies?—Capulet, Montague, / See what a scourge is laid upon your hate, / That heaven finds means to kill your joys with love, / And I, for winking at your discords too, / Have lost a brace of kinsmen. All are punished." (V. 3. 301-305.)

Capulet responds, "O brother Montague, give me thy hand. / This is my daughter's jointure, for no more / Can I demand." (V. 3. 306—308.)

Montague replies, "But I can give thee more, / For I will ray her statue in pure gold, / That whiles Verona by that name is known, / There shall no figure at such rate be set / As that of true and faithful Juliet." (V. 3. 309—131.)

The play ends with a summation by the Prince and the final lines of the play: "For never was a story of more woe / Than this of Juliet and her Romeo." (V. 3. 320—321.)

As with all the other scenes of the play, these final scenes bring together characters at the height of their emotions. The plot also advances the story to its *fulfillment*, that the love of Romeo and Juliet is so great as to defy even death and reunite their families.

The great storytelling craft of *Romeo and Juliet* reveals why Shakespeare is rightly renowned as one of the great artists of all time.

Chapter Questions

In what way do you give your story a sense of dramatic passion that will engage the interest of your audience?

In what ways do your characters speak with passion about their feelings?

In what way does your story create a richness of feelings similar to those expressed in this play?

When you read your stories, do you feel emotionally moved and thoughtfully engaged?

When your characters are in dramatic, desperate situations, do you feel caught up in the drama you've created?

The Art of Creating Drama

A Review of 'night, Mother

Written by Marsha Norman. Available in paperback from Noonday Press, a division of Farrar, Straus and Giroux. ISBN: 0374521387. Can be purchased from Amazon.com or through book stores. The play won a Pulitzer Prize for Drama in 1983. It is also available as a film and on audio cassette. Page numbers used for citations are from the Noonday Press edition of the play.

'night, Mother by Marsha Norman is a brilliant play.

This story explores the life of Jessie Cates who lives with her mother, Thelma. The play opens with Jessie asking her mother where a particular gun is kept. She finds it with Thelma's help. As she cleans the gun, she quietly announces she's going to kill herself at the end of the evening. Jessie's announcement sets off a fierce struggle between mother and daughter, with Thelma using every strategy she can conceive of to talk Jessie out of her plan. Thelma becomes so desperate, she resorts to telling Jessie the truth about a number of issues that have affected her life.

The play illustrates a central facet of what creates drama in a story: the anticipation of an outcome for a dramatic issue. In this case, that means that Thelma and the story's audience learn early on of Jessie's plans, and they are therefore thrust deep into the heart of a story question: Will Jessie really kill herself, or can Thelma find a way to stop her?

What's at stake in this story is made chillingly clear.

Of all the many issues that bedevil the inexperienced writer, one of the more damaging is the myth that one creates drama by withholding information. In 'night, Mother, the more reasons Thelma offers to convince Jessie not to kill herself, the more she reaffirms Jessie's belief that her life is useless, that it's simply better to end her suffering with a clear mind.

By setting up her story question so concretely, the playwright uses the situation to compel Thelma into what is for her completely unexplored territory: her own heart. What follows is a review of the play's structure and how it makes concrete Thelma's journey to a dark, bitter illumination.

'night, Mother

The play opens on what appears to be a typical Saturday night for Jessie, a woman in her late thirties to early forties, and her mother Thelma. Thelma finds the last snowball—some junk food—in the fridge. Jessie asks for some black plastic bags. It's on their schedule that Jessie give Thelma a manicure. All are the events of a routine, predictable evening between Jessie and Thelma. Then (Noonday Press edition of the play), Jessie asks, "Where's Daddy's gun?" (Page 7.)

Life for Jessie and Thelma is such a dull routine, Thelma doesn't even pause to consider the request odd. She even helps Jessie figure out where the gun is kept. It's only a few minutes later that Thelma asks, "What do you want the gun for, Jess?" (Page 9.) "Protection," answers Jessie.

With the introduction of Jessie's question about the location of the gun, the playwright began setting the hook for her story question.

Thelma at first considers that she and Jessie have nothing worth stealing because what was valuable was stolen by Jessie's son, Ricky. Thelma says, "I mean, I don't even want what we got, Jessie." (Page 10.)

This conversation about what Jessie might be seeking protection from provides information about the other characters in her life, principally Ricky.

Jessie begins cleaning the gun. By page twelve, the stage directions state that Thelma is now concerned about the gun and asks why Jessie wants it. Jessie replies, "The gun is for me." (Page 13.) Thelma says, "Well, you can have it if you want. When I die, you'll get it anyway." (Page 13.) Jessie says, "I'm going to kill myself, Mama."

The hook of this story has just been set.

At first Thelma upbraids Jessie for her bad "joke," but Jessie patiently insists she's serious. Thelma then insists the gun won't work, the bullets are fifteen years old. Jessie tells her that Dawson, her brother, told her where to buy new bullets. As Jessie describes Dawson's enthusiasm to tell her about bullets, the playwright has found an avenue to introduce a major, if unseen, character. Thelma threatens to call Dawson, to have him come and take the gun away. This leads Jessie to insist that if Thelma makes the call, she'll kill herself before Dawson can get there, and she and Thelma won't have their last evening alone together. Jessie says, "I'm through talking, Mama. You're it. No more." (Page 17.)

Thelma responds that in all likelihood, Jessie will only shoot off her ear and turn herself into a vegetable. This is an important exchange, because it sets the story on a course of exploring the emotional terrain of both Jessie's life and her life with her mother. From the moment Jessie makes her announcement about her impending suicide, everything about that terrain stands in bold relief.

Thelma continues trying to find something that will give her leverage over Jessie. That Jessie can't use her towels when she kills herself, that she can't use the gun because Jessie's father gave it to Thelma. She then switches tactics, trying to find out why Jessie wants to kill herself. This continues the story's exploration of Jessie's life and her relationship with her mother. All of this minutia is given dramatic weight because of Jessie's promise. Finally Jessie says, "And I can't do anything either, about my life, to change it, make it better, make me feel better about it. Like it better, make it work. But I can stop it. Shut it down, turn it off like the radio when there's nothing on I want to listen to." (Page 36.)

This is delightful dialogue, spare, evocative, tightly written. It cuts to the heart of Jessie's reasons for wanting to die.

In the next series of exchanges, it is revealed why a friend of Thelma's refuses to come into her house. She's seen the death in Jessie's eyes. This revelation of Jessie's intentions is a potent way for the playwright to use what's at stake for Jessie—her life or death—to explore the reality of Jessie's life. For probably the first time ever in her relationship with her daughter, Thelma begins to speak a deeper truth to Jessie.

This new dialogue leads Jessie to ask whether her mother ever loved her father. Again, Thelma speaks a truth she's never voiced before. It leads to the revelation that Thelma suspects Jessie's father also suffered from the seizures that have plagued Jessie's life. The secrets Thelma has kept from Jessie spill out in a torrent. That Jessie's father never really went fishing. Instead, he'd just sit by a lake in his car. Until this night, Thelma had created an almost impenetrable surface of meaningless chat that only Jessie's impending death has been able to breach.

Jessie and Thelma next talk about Jessie's ex-husband who Thelma had conspired to introduce to her. During the marriage, Jessie fell off a horse. The accident was thought to have led to her seizure disorder. But one of the truths that is uncovered is that Jessie began having seizures as a child, but Thelma covered it up. It was something she didn't want to think about, so she found a way to simply go on. Thelma explains, "I don't like things to think about. I like things to go on." (Page 52.)

As Jessie talks about her former husband, another area of her life comes into stark relief. Again, the playwright has found a way to use Jessie's impending death to give each revelation about her life a quality of clarity.

When it is revealed that because of her medication Jessie can now think more clearly, Thelma jumps on that as a reason to live. But for Jessie, the medication had another effect. "If I'd ever had a year like this, to think straight and all, before now, I'd be gone already," she says. (Page 68.)

As the time nears for the night to be over, Thelma tries in desperation to find some way to forestall Jessie. "I didn't tell you things or I married you off to the wrong man or I took you in and let your life get away from you or all of it put together." (Page 72.) But as that final moment of Jessie's life draws near, Thelma becomes calm and pliant. She simply accepts that Jessie will end her life. She repeats to Jessie her suggestions about what Thelma should say to the people who come to Jessie's funeral.

Jessie goes into her room to do the deed. Thelma collapses and cries out, "Jessie! Please!" (Page 89.) The gunshot answers with a sound like "no." (Page 89.)

Thelma, "Jessie, Jessie, child...Forgive me. (pause) I thought you were mine." (Page 89.) Thelma, following Jessie's instructions, goes to the phone and calls her son Dawson.

This is a profoundly moving play. The principle that I want to point out one last time is that it develops its drama not from hiding what's at stake— Jessie's impending death—but by setting it out in a way the storyteller develops drama around the outcome of the question: will Jessie kill herself?

It is the nature of drama that one can only have a story if there's a cause behind what sets the story into motion. *night, Mother* is an example of where something blunt and obvious—Jessie's impending death—can give dramatic meaning to mundane events such as making cocoa and eating a caramel apple. The storyteller who fails to set up an issue that connects with an audience risks assembling words and images to no purpose. By making what's at stake in this story clear and direct, the storyteller frees herself to begin the real task that faces every storyteller:

Bringing an audience fully into and involved with the world these story characters inhabit

'night, Mother is a great example of the art of creating a potent, dramatic story by early on revealing what's at stake and steadily increasing the tension around a situation characters are driven to resolve.

Chapter Questions

How do you introduce what's at stake in your story as a story question?

How do you introduce this question in a way that ensures your audience will care about the outcome?

How does your plot operate to increase the dramatic pressure on both your characters and your audience?

How does the plot of your story force your characters into a territory of new feelings and new truths about themselves?

Setting a Story into Motion

A Review of *The Exorcist*

Written by William Blatty. Reissued as a Harper Mass Market Paperback 1994. ISBN: 0553270109. Also available on audio cassette (unabridged) through Amazon.com. Page citations in the following text are from the hardcover edition of the book published by Harper and Row.

For many writers, the issue of how to structure the elements of a novel can seem a mystery only to be solved by writing a novel and seeing where it goes. Another path is to review a well-written novel to understand its structure. What follows is a review of the opening pages of *The Exorcist*.

William Blatty begins setting out the dramatic purpose of his story on the first page of his prologue. In the opening paragraph, Blatty writes: "He could not shake the premonition. It clung to his back like chill wet leaves." (Page 3.)

What this premonition is and why it clings to the narrator's back is revealed latter. To get the answer to the question posed by these two sentences, the story's audience must continue reading.

Note that Blatty has already given his audience a place for the location of the prologue simply by having a title page that reads: "Prologue: Northern Iraq."

This is a subtle but important point. An audience beginning a story desires to know where and when the story is happening. Blatty satisfies that need in the simplest, most direct way possible. Continuing, Blatty lets us know that we are at an archeological dig in Iraq.

In the second paragraph of the prologue Blatty writes: "The bones of man.

The brittle remnants of cosmic torment that once made him wonder if matter was Lucifer upward-groping back to his God. And yet now he knew better." (Page 3.)

Blatty just cued his audience that the drama of this story will revolve around good and evil, Lucifer, God, and humankind. He also sets up another question: What is this issue the narrator now "knew better?" It is a suggestive comment that both sets up the story's dramatic purpose while drawing the reader deeper into the story to discover the answer.

At the end of the second paragraph, the author writes: "The dig was over. What was beginning?" (Page 3.) The author informs the audience through the story's narrator that significant events are taking shape.

Note that at the end of the second paragraph, we know more about the story than we do about the character perceiving these events. Blatty, like most successful novelists, has not confused introducing character and plot with introducing his story. If he'd simply found a way to introduce his characters and plot but not his story, the actions of his characters would lack dramatic purpose.

In the third paragraph, a "dark shadow" appears over the prologue's narrator. These words are suggestive of the forces that will be unleashed in this story.

Looking at the dirt-encrusted shoes of a local helping with the dig, the narrator thinks, "The man in khaki shook his head, staring down at the laceless, crusted shoes caked thick with debris of the pain of living." (Page 4.)

The author continues to alert his audience to his story's dramatic purpose via the details he chooses to describe. Continuing: "The stuff of the cosmos, he softly reflected: matter, yet somehow spirit. Spirit and the shoes were to him but aspects of a stuff more fundamental, a stuff that was primal and totally other." (Page 4.)

This story will explore not just what is visible, but also this "other" that underlies reality.

The author continues: "The shadow lifted. The Kurd stood waiting like an ancient debt....Once he could not have loved this man." (Page 4.)

This last line is a very suggestive. If "once he could not have loved this man," then what happened to our narrator? Again there's the arrangement of the story's elements designed to pull its audience deeper into the story. Note that as yet we don't know the narrator's name, how old he is, or his background.

The man takes out his wallet and an out of date calendar card with a Jesuit saying comes into view, "What we give to the poor is what we take with us when we die." (Page 4.)

We now know this man has an association with the Jesuits, and the words on this card also speak to the dramatic purpose of this story.

The next paragraph begins, "The leaves clutched tighter at his back. Something was waiting." (Page 4.)

It is direct, to the point, and chilling. It introduces a premonition, an escalation of the dramatic effect of the premonition.

With the departure of the narrator, the author switches for a moment to the Kurd, who feels "strangely alone." That in the narrator's presence he felt "something like safety." Again, these are statements that raise a question about what it was that frightened the Kurd so that he felt safe in the Jesuit's presence? To get the answer to yet another question, you must keep reading.

In the next scene, the narrator meets with a curator in Mosul. The Arab narrator of the scene notes that the Jesuit who remains nameless now holds an amulet that called forth a demon for protection. The curator says that he wishes the Jesuit were not going home to the States. Notice how this sets up the Jesuit's likely destination in an effortless way that also raises a question, Will the Jesuit stay or return to the States? Leaving the curator and his shop, our Jesuit is almost run over by a cart driven by an Arab woman whose veil is "draped loosely over her face like a shroud." Again the telling detail that ties in with the story's purpose of exploring the boundaries of life and death, good and evil.

The narrator soon leaves the city. "Nearing the ruins, he slowed his pace, for with every step the inchoate presentiment took firmer, more horrible form." (Page 7.)

Note the escalation of his premonition. First the premonition was a chill; now it looms more dangerously. This author never repeats his points. He gives them greater depth of meaning by offering new information. The author continues, setting out the thought of the Jesuit father: "Yet he had to know. He would have to prepare." (Page 7.)

Have to know what? Prepare for what? Again, we must keep reading without slackening our pace. Also note that the audience is firmly cued to the idea that what he must prepare for is a battle between good and evil. That was made clear in the opening of the prologue. Now the shape that battle will take is becoming clearer and more concrete. Again, this is an example of a story's movement as it advances along its story line.

The narrator steps into what was once Nineveh, an ancient, feared city. Standing among the ancient ruins, he has a potent premonition that: "And yet he was here, the air was still thick with him, the 'other' who ravished his dreams." (Page 7.)

Very dramatic. Who is this other? We still don't know this man's name and what he looks like, but we do know we're caught up in a dangerous battle between good and evil.

He finds a statue of the demon Pazuzu, and the narrator comes to a realization that staggers him:

"Abruptly he sagged. He knew. It was coming." (Page 7.)

This is *scary*. But note, the above lines are suggestive; they don't tell us what is coming, just that it is evil. This is great foreshadowing.

The author writes: "The orb of the sun was beginning to fall below the rim of the world." (Page 7.) A prologue that begins in the blistering heat of day ends with the approach of night. A night that will see the return of something very dark and evil to the world.

The prologue ends with the words: "He hastened toward Mosul and his train, his heart encased in the icy conviction that soon he would face an ancient enemy." (Page 7.)

We still don't know this man's name but we know what's looming in the darkness that he must face. The prologue took us from a premonition to the narrator's journey to Nineveh where his premonition is clarified and made concrete. What this evil will look like is left for a later revelation, but that it will manifest itself is assured.

A subtle but vital point, without this establishing of this beginning of a battle between good and evil, details about Jesuit as a character at a dig in Iraq would not set the story into motion. Blatty took great pains to introduce his audience to his story as early as possible.

One comes away from this prologue knowing a story about a battle between good and evil has been set into motion.

A second vital point to note is that within those first six pages Blatty, establishes strong narrative tension around his narrator. By that I mean that his narrator clearly feels he must battle this evil coming into the world; it's a fight he cannot walk away from.

Another point worth remembering is that a novel is created with both a story line and a plot line. Via his prologue, Blatty introduces a story about this conflict between good and evil. By the time one has finished reading the six-page prologue, one has already advanced six pages into the story along its story line.

The plot line of the story begins when the narrator finds the amulet at an ancient site in Iraq and realizes it is a concrete manifestation of an evil returning to the world. Up until the opening scene of the story, he'd only had premonitions about the return of that evil manifesting itself. That heightening of tension is the purpose of a novel's plot. By page six, one is six pages into the story and six pages along its plot line.

Blatty has carefully constructed the opening of the novel so that it has a beginning to its story line interwoven with his plot line. And the story will be acted out by a character determined to resolve what's at stake in the story.

Blatty also takes great care to make sure each moment of his prologue is dramatic, written to create an anticipation of an outcome. A novel can be considered a series of dramatic moments. Understanding the larger dramatic purpose of the story, its story question and story line and plot line, Blatty had a clear focus on the dramatic purpose of each moment in the prologue. His writing always serves to heighten the dramatic effect of each of those moments in a way that contributes to the overall dramatic effect of the story and its advance along its story line.

This author displays an excellent understanding of the craft of writing a novel.

Chapter Questions

Is the promise and dramatic purpose of your novel clear from its opening pages, scenes, and chapter?

Do your opening scenes both introduce your story and set it into motion along its story line and plot line?

What are you doing to create a sense of narrative tension around the actions of your main character?

What are you doing to help transfer that narrative tension from your main character to your audience?

The Artist as Storyteller

A Review of *City of Glass*

Written by Paul Auster. Published by Penguin USA (paper-back). ISBN: 0140097317. Full title: City of Glass (The New York Trilogy, Vol 1). Available through Amazon.com and book stores.

What makes a novel the work of an artist? My answer is that an artist is concerned not just with how a story's movement affects an audience—creating an action story that thrills, for example—but with *why* an audience desires particular experiences from stories. The artistic storyteller uses a story to illuminate some aspect of the artist's own world and the overall human condition.

A question I'm asked is, are the principles an artist uses to create a story the same as those that apply to more simple, popular stories? My answer is yes.

The purpose of this review is to break down, sentence by sentence, the opening page of a novella, *City of Glass*, written by an artist—Paul Auster. Following that review, I'll explore how the opening page of the novella sets up the story's issues and promise in a way that is resolved in an artistic, thoughtful manner.

City of Glass opens with, "It was a wrong number that started it, the telephone ringing three times in the dead of night, and the voice on the other end asking for someone he was not." This sentence raises a number of questions. Who is the narrator who knew it was a wrong number? What did this phone call "start?" Who is this someone "who was not?" This first sentence is constructed to entice its audience into the world of this story. Note that while the sentence raises a number of questions, it does not take the form of a question.

"Much later, when he was able to think about the things that happened to him, he would conclude that nothing was real except chance." In this second sentence we are told that an element of this story will revolve around chance and the nature of reality. This is the story's promise. Note how quickly the artist orients his audience to a dramatic purpose for his story; it is not withheld to create a revelation.

First the audience is deftly, quickly eased into the story, and then the third sentence, "But that was much later," tells us that the narrator of this story has gone on a journey, and the phone call in the middle of the night was its beginning. This sentence foretells that more information will emerge later about the nature of both the phone call, this idea of chance, and the nature of reality. The audience must keep reading to find out what these revelations will be.

"In the beginning, there was simply the event and its consequences." Even though the writer slips the phrase, "In the beginning…," into this fourth sentence, we're already deep into the beginning of the story. The phrase, "there was simply the event and its consequences," speaks on one level about plot in a story—this happened, so that happened. This fourth sentence offers a kind of Newtonian world view—event and consequence—that the author will re-examine through the telling of this story.

The artist further defines the terrain this story explores when he says, "Whether it might have turned out differently, or whether it was all predetermined with the first word that came from the stranger's mouth, is not the question." He is telling the audience that this story and its outcome *will not* turn on a simple examination of events in a Newtonian world that operates via cause and effect. This artist intends to take his audience on a penetrating journey of exploring chance and reality. Again, Auster writes to set out his dramatic purpose, not conceal it.

In the sixth sentence, "The question is the story itself, and whether it means something is not for the story to tell," a judgment about a story is being made by its observer as well as its artist-creator. The audience is reminded that it is a participant in the story and its meaning. This is a view that explores a reality different from a Newtonian one.

This first paragraph has done its job of drawing the reader in. It is beautifully written, and each sentence has a clear, direct dramatic purpose. Each sentence communicates that this is a story about the nature of chance and reality.

The second paragraph begins, "As for Quinn, there is little that need detail us." This is a beautiful introduction to a character, giving us a name and telling us there's no real reason to pay attention. Which guarantees, of course, that the reader pays even *more* attention.

Note how the narrator of the story casually slips into a confidence with the story's audience when he says, "is little that need detail *us*." (Italics added.) The audience has become a participant with the author in observing the events of the story.

In the second sentence, "Who he was, where he came from, and what he did are of no great importance," the artist cleverly plays off the common understanding of how to introduce a character in a way that leads the audience to care about the character's goals and issues. Auster confounds that expectation in a way that leads to the audience to want to know more about what we're told we don't need to know. And the audience asks the deeper questions—why don't we need to know more about this character? What's the author up to? We have to keep reading to find out. The paragraph continues, "We know, for example, that he was thirty-five years old."

Who is this "we" who "knows" about Quinn? By not asking a question, the artist implicitly asks a question. Similarly, the artist coyly pulls us deeper into the story with, "We know, for example, that he had once been married, had once been a father, and that both wife and son were now dead." Auster has hooked us with the question of this being a story about chance and the nature of reality, and now he's offering us information in an off-hand way about a character we're told is not important. Personally, I have to keep reading to find out what Quinn does or doesn't have to do with this story.

When we read the next sentence, "We also know that he wrote books," it's hard to escape the "aha" factor. Is the author letting us know in a sly way that this "unimportant" Quinn is his stand-in? Again, we have to keep reading as the mystery around Quinn and who he is deepens with every sentence that assures us he's of no consequence.

In the sixth sentence, Auster writes, "To be precise, we know that he wrote mystery novels." Of course. What better setting for a story about the mystery of chance and reality than a narrator who writes mystery novels? It will be a natural meditation for him.

"Those works were written under the name of William Wilson, and he produced them at the rate of about one a year, which brought in enough money for him to live modestly in a small New York apartment." This sentence both introduces a question—why William Wilson?—while easing away from an other potential area of inquiry, how does the narrator maintain his living standard. Since our narrator has no need for money, he won't be pressed by this common issue. The sentence also gives the story a place, New York.

The story continues, "Because he spent no more than five or six months on a novel, for the rest of the year he was free do as he wished." In other words, Quinn has the time to become absorbed in the story's mystery. "He read many books, he looked at paintings, he went to the movies."

"In the summer he watched baseball on television; in the winter he went to the opera." Again, by suggesting the details of this character's life are unimportant, the author finds a clever way to give them a sheen of importance.

However, with the next sentence, "More than anything else, however, what he liked to do was walk," we feel we are being set up for another revelation. "Nearly every day, rain or shine, hot or cold, he would leave his apartment to walk through the city, never going anywhere, but simply going wherever his legs happened to take him." This concludes the "simple" introduction of Quinn, the unimportant man, and is the last sentence of the first page.

In the rest of the chapter, we're told that through walking without volition, Quinn could bring himself to a state of emptiness. In the past, Quinn had not been so empty, but he'd given up on the personality he'd been born with to let William Wilson, the writer, be his public self. "Quinn continued to exist, he no longer existed for anyone but himself." Quinn, through William Wilson, keeps the world at a distance. Quinn even stops dreaming. Then comes the night of the opening sentence, the phone call. The caller is someone looking to speak to Paul Auster, of the Auster Detective Agency.

The hook for this story has been set. The terrain for the story is now clear. Later, at the end of the first chapter, the unidentified caller phones again, and this time Quinn says that *he* is Paul Auster, the detective, to find out more about the caller. The caller professes that someone means to kill someone, and only Paul Auster can help.

We are given almost no choice but to turn the page and start reading chapter two. The search for answers to this story's probing questions must continue.

Along with its artistic vision, this opening chapter is organized around the principles of storytelling used to write stories about more conventional situations. It opens with a question that pulls the reader in, who is the caller? It broadens to, who is Quinn? It broadens again to, what is the relationship among Quinn the narrator, Auster the fictional detective, and Auster the novella's creator? Who is this person who will be killed without Auster's intervention?Unlike the a more conventional story, Auster creates revelations around a layered texture of drama. Drama that revolves around the nature of reality as it is expressed through chance and how a fragment of the receiver's personality must deal with a perception of an event.

Auster draws us into this world with great skill and clarity of purpose.

In chapter two, Quinn, as Paul Auster, the fictional detective, meets the caller, the wife of the husband she fears will be murdered by his father who's being released from prison. She seeks to hire Auster/Wilson/Quinn to protect her husband. But this is merely the surface of the story. Auster the storyteller sets out a deeper, more complex world. The son Quinn is hired to protect has been raised by his father as part of an experiment to find a way to return to a pre-tower-of-Babel world. A world where every "thing" in the world has a fixed, understandable meaning that can be expressed in a pure language.

On a certain level, it's a call for a return to the world of Newton, where one can confidently speak about the world as a kind of cosmic clock—if you understand the mechanism, you can predict events. Writing a story that revolves around these characters, Auster takes his audience into a deeper mystery than what will be the outcome of this "case." The real mystery of the story revolves around the author illuminating ideas about the nature of reality, personality, and chance, a world that exists outside of the Newtonian framework.

In the story, the narrator becomes obsessed with the mystery of why the father wants to kill his son, and also with the old man and his ideas about the nature of reality. But the deeper the detective Auster/Quinn/Wilson becomes absorbed and obsessed with finding the "truth" about the old man's intentions, the more bereft he becomes of finding any kind of truth about what's been happening in the story. By the end of the novel, Auster the novella's creator appears as a character. Even more illuminating, the actions of Auster the author are taken to task by a character who serves as kind of an over-soul, one who sits in judgment on the activities of Auster and the characters in the world he's created.

This final frame for the novella creates a continuum that reveals a relationship between the fragment of the author (Paul Auster) who creates the fragments of characters (Quinn, the old man) who act in a way that creates a kind of fragmented truth for the story's audience about the story's meaning. This story beautifully explores the modern day terrain of what it means to live in an age where so many people live fragmented lives. At each stage of the story, the audience is taken not only further toward the resolution of the story's surface mystery, but also into an examination of the role of chance upon the formation of fragments of personality. Each chapter takes us through a corresponding series of revelations that both resolve the story's mystery while exploring the nature of personality.

This story's plot takes the reader into a story world composed of a perception of events designed to make the reader a participant in the story In much the same way, when Auster the author becomes a character in the story, he also becomes a fragment of his own personality.

Breaking down and diagramming this story would reveal not only a series of events, but also allow for an examination of the ideas that underlie the telling of the story itself. This, again, is the prime difference between the storyteller as artist and the writer of popular fiction. The artist creates a story-world that asks his audience to explore its own thoughts and perceptions as part of experiencing the story. Where a mundane story would ask, who's the murderer, etc., Auster asks, what's the nature of the self that asks these questions? That difference in focus and intent is a prime difference between art and popular entertainment. Auster is both an artist and a storyteller, a brilliant writer who is a joy to read.

Chapter Questions

What questions about the meaning of life does your story raise?

What illuminations about life does your story offer?

How does your story take on a depth of dramatic purpose as it advances?

Do you see the characters in your stories as reflections of you? If so, how does that affect what kind of stories you write?

Do you ever want to become a character in your stories? Why, or why not?

Give Me A Dramatic Truth
Or Give Me Death!

A Review of Afterlife

Screenplay written by Kore-eda Hirokau. Directed by
Kore-eda Hirokau. Starring: Aarata, Erike Oda, Sususma
Terajima, Taketoshi Naito. Released in 1998. On video.

A Japanese film, *After Life*, directed by Kore-eda Hirokazu, speaks to characters
embodying dramatic truths. This artful story has a simple opening. Two young
men are talking. One complains about an old man talking incessantly about sex
for three days before he 'chose a vacation with his wife.' They reach a forlorn
office and a manager mentions they sent '18 through' the previous week, but,
this week they have a heavier load. Then, as a bell rings, people enter from the
fog into a non-descript building. It's a simple, beautifully staged scene. The
people who entered the building are then individually called into interview
rooms and we learn that these people have died. As we cut betwee different
interviews, we get the answer to the 'why' of this place. Each person has three
days to choose a memory that they will take withthem into the after life, and
that memory will be filmed and ready to take with them within a week.

What memory will they choose?

The question offers a look into the dramatic truths of their lives.
What single event had the most meaning to them? The story is staged so the
audience gets to share the dramatic journey toward these answers. It's a

dramatic journey for reasons that soon become clear. Some people can't, or refuse, to make up their minds in the three days they have to make a decision. This puts pressure on the people doing the interviews, and the audience.

When a story's audience has internalized the tension over a story's course and outcome, that audience desires to experience the journey toward a story's resolution and fulfillment. When an audience desires and needs the completion of a story's journey for the relief of narrative tension it offers, that story will hold the attention of an audience. Every element of this film is designed to naturally and quietly draw us into this story's world.

One of the first people to be interviewed is a man who only has bad memories. He adds that if he'd lived longer, he only would have accumulated more bad memories. This is the dramatic truth of his life.

A young man quickly wants the rules of the road set out. Is there a hell that people are sent to? When he learns the answer is no, he responds that he has no intention of choosing a memory.

It becomes apparent that an old man is also struggling to pick a memory. He wants diaries to help him decide, pictures of his past life.

An old, old, moon-faced lady who seems to be deaf goes out collecting leaves, nuts, and twigs from the grounds of the land surrounding this place. She asks why there aren't any flowers. The interviewer answers that they bloom in the spring, a revelation that even this place has seasons. It comes out that the old lady has regressed and sees the world as a nine year old. A subtle, potent dramatic truth about her that is unexpected.

It also comes out that the people running this facility have video tapes of people's lives they can use to help prompt people to chose a memory. On his video tape, the old man struggling to choose a memory watches himself speak about a dramatic truth of his life, that as a young man he wants 'evidence' that he's been alive, that his life has had meaning.

We continue with other interviews. The man with painful memories realizes if he just has to pick one memory, he won't have to remember all the other painful memories of his life. This scene is staged from behind the man, with the camera on the faces on two interviewers to his left and right. The image is beautifully composed. Nothing distracts the audience from taking in this man's sad dramatic truth.

It is the job of the screenwriter to suggest dramatic truths that lend themselves to being acted out in a potent, visual ways. Scripts that lack revelations of dramatic truths become recitations of what things look like. It's not a question of being overly descriptive, but of choosing words and images that have the maximum impact on a reader. Novelists must choose scenes that put both characters and their audience into deeper states of feeling, illumination of ideas, or just the feeling of being on a roller coaster.

Two interviewers, a young man and woman, join the old man struggling to pick a memory. As the old man watches scenes with his wife from an arranged marriage, the look on the face of the young man interviewer tells us there's something significant about the woman he sees on the screen. The young man then asks the manager to be taken off the case. This sets up a major, heartfelt revelation. This young man was once engaged to the young, vivacious woman the old man married when he was young.

The old man finally makes his choice after viewing a moment in his life spent on a park bench bantering with his playful wife about how often they will go out to watch movies.

He apologizes for taking so long to make up his mind and we get another major revelation. The interviewers are people who couldn't choose one memory to take with them into the after life. Until they decide, they must interview others. The dramatic truth of this situation is that listening to others long enough eventually leads these interviewers to make their own choices.

As the dead choose after life memories, their memories are filmed. This filmmaking is on a par with a low-budget film, adding to the charm of the story. Cotton balls pass for clouds. Cherry blossoms glide around the moon-faced old lady. An old woman has to teach a little girl a dance for her favorite memory. When the memories of the week are filmed, the deceased file into a viewing room to watch them. Meanwhile, the young male interviewer goes to take the videotapes from the old man's room. He finds a note from the old man explaining that he came to realize the young man was the fiancée of his wife before she met him. He explains in his note that his wife clearly cherished the memory of this young man. That through meeting this young man in the after life, the old man came to understand the meaning of his life and the time he spent with his wife.

The young man protests to another young woman interviewer that he deeply regrets that he never had the easy familiarity that the old man shared with his fiancée, and that this wounds him deeply. The young woman then shows him the memory that his fiancée choose to take into her after life. It's her and her young fiance sitting on a park bench, the young man stiff and uncomfortable. The young man is clearly amazed that his fiancé choose this memory to take into the after life. He says, "I searched desperately inside myself, for any memory of happiness. Now, fifty years later, I've learned, I was part of someone else's happiness. What a wonderful discovery. You, too, someday will find this." She insists she won't ever leave this place, because to leave this place would be to leave the memory of her love for him. The young man vows he'll never forget her.

He asks that he be allowed to take into the after life his realization about his young fiancé. The manager of the facility then affirms that they'll make an exception and let the young man take his realization of what he discovered about himself sitting on that park bench on the set of the old man's memory. That memory is then filmed.

The young man then sits in the viewing station with the young woman. His filmed memory includes his looking out and seeing the people filming his memory, including the young woman. When the clip finishes and the lights come up, the young man has disappeared, moved on to the after life with his memory.

We end with another group of the newly deceased coming in out of the fog and the young woman, alone, practicing the questions she needs to ask until she hears the door to the interview room open.

This film is great, joyful, rich storytelling. What makes this movie special aren't big effects or beautiful Hollywood actors or lavish sets, but a simple journey into the hearts of the story's characters and the dramatic truths found there.

That is a story where each character has to come to understand the dramatic truth of their lives before they can pass on.

Chapter Questions

What dramatic truths do your main characters embody?

How do they resolve these truths? Fulfill them?

Conscious Storytelling

A Review of Memento

Screenplay by Christopher Nolan. Directed by
Christopher Nolan. Starring: Guy Pearce, Carrie-Anne
Moss, Joe Pantoliano, Mark Boone. Released in 2001.
Available on video.

Introducing a story's promise in a dramatic context – in a way that suggests a
need for the resolution - sets a story into motion.

A question I'm asked is, does suggesting the promise of a story make a
beginning too obvious? It can. The obvious can also become a starting point to
find a suggestive, elusive, engaging opening that still speaks to a story's deeper
purpose.

Memento, written and directed by Christopher Nolan, is a story that suggests Nolan understands the craft of storytelling. Memento starts with someone waving a picture of a man shot to death. The time sequence goes backwards,
with the picture fading out and being withdrawn into a camera. The blood
from the shooting returns to the dead man, who comes back to life.

This opening suggests the story will go back in time. The opening also
raises questions: who is the man with the camera, why did he shoot the dead
man?

We go back in time to get these answers. The man with the camera, Lenny,
is meeting with Teddy, the dead man. Lenny explains to Teddy that he has a
handicap as they drive to the scene of Teddy's death. When they arrive at a
deserted industrial location, Lenny goes into a building. He takes out a photo
of Teddy with a note on it to 'not believe Teddy's lies, that he should kill Teddy.'
Lenny then turns on Teddy with a gun. Teddy

should kill Teddy.' Lenny then turns on Teddy with a gun. Teddy protests that Lenny only knows who he used to be, not what he has become; and that if Lenny wants the truth about himself, it's in the basement. We then we cut back to a hotel room where Lenny explains to someone on the phone that 'Sammy Jenkins' had no system like Lenny. Who Sammy Jenkins is and what is Lenny's 'system' sets up new questions. Lenny explains his 'handicap' to a clerk, that he can no longer retain new memories since his wife's death and his being struck on the head. That answers a question, why Lenny takes photos, but doesn't explain why Lenny killed Teddy. The audience is always being drawn forward, scene by scene.

Next scene, Lenny tells the hotel clerk he doesn't want to see Teddy. Then Teddy shows up. We see on Lenny's wrist the note, 'Remember Sammy Jenkins.' Lenny tattoos information he wants to remember onto his body. That's part of his 'system.'

Going back in time again, we see a car registration with Teddy's photo and the name John Gamol. Lenny then takes off his shirt. Tattooed on his chest is a message that his wife was raped and murdered by a man named John G. What's important to Lenny, his story, he tattoos on his body, in the same way people are self-branded with ideas or feelings about their lives. In Memento, Nolan finds a creative way to make that impulse larger than life.

Lenny writes on Teddy's photo that Teddy killed his wife.

The story then cuts to Lenny on the phone telling someone the story of Sammy Jenkins. Cutting to this story-within-a-story happens throughout the film. Lenny was an insurance adjustor who turned down a claim by Sammy, who suffered a brain injury that left him unable to form new memories. When Lenny tells Sammy's wife that Sammy's problem is mental, she ultimately challenges this by asking Sammy to repeatedly give her insulin shots. If he's 'faking' and he loves her, he won't do something that could lead to her death. But he does. The quest of Sammy Jenkin's wife to discover the truth about her husband gives these scenes dramatic tension, while also giving the audience information about Lenny's condition.

Lenny goes to meet Natalie. He's written on her photo that she's helping him because she also lost someone. Natalie has a split lip and a black eye, which raises the question, who hit her? Natalie is the one who gave Lenny the information that ID'd Teddy as John Gamol. This explains why Lenny thinks Teddy killed his wife. Natalie asks Lenny to tell her what he remembers about his wife. As Lenny tells Natalie about his wife, this helps the audience 'feel' why Lenny is so driven on his quest to avenge her death.

As we go back in time, Teddy tells Lenny that Natalie is trying to set Lenny up to kill the wrong man. Who's lying? Teddy or Natalie? Or both? Why? We continue back in time to get the answers.

Lenny wakes up in bed with Natalie, who he doesn't recognize. She kisses Lenny and asks that he at least remember that, but it's clear he won't.

We then cut to the night before. Lenny arrives at Natalie's demanding to know 'who Dodd' is. He's a man with a bloody face in a photo Lenny took. Natalie reveals that she lost someone named Jimmy, that he went to meet Teddy about a drug deal and never came back. When Lenny sees a picture of Natalie and Jimmy together, he writes on a photo of her that she's lost someone.

We go back in time one more step, and Lenny wakes up to find himself in a hotel room with a man with a bloody face, Dodd, tied up in a closet. Teddy shows up and wants to know what's happening, but Lenny can't remember. But, because the story is going backwards in time, the audience knows they'll get the answer. Even with the time sequence reversed, the audience is always allowed a sense of scene to scene continuity, of being moved toward the answer to a question raised in a previous scene.

We then go back in time again to Lenny in a shower and hearing someone enter the hotel room. Lenny gets in a fight with Dodd and knocks him out with a bottle of liquor. Lenny then ties up Dodd, puts him into a closet, takes his picture, writes himself a note to get rid of Dodd, ask Natalie about Dodd, then Lenny calls Teddy.

We then go back in time, and Lenny is running in a trailer court. Lenny's already forgotten whether he's chasing someone or running from someone. He then comes across Dodd, who shoots at him, which answers the question of whether Lenny is the pursuer or the pursued. This was my favorite scene in the movie. The set up is perfect.

We go back again, showing Dodd originally trying to kill Lenny, which raises the question, why? Again we have an immediate and clear question that will be answered by going back in time. Because the story is like a puzzle piece, every scene must have a specific purpose, a specific shape and design.

The scenes continue to be intercut with Lenny on the phone talking with someone (we later discover is Teddy) about some missing pages in the police report about his wife's death. It comes out that the police suspected a drug dealer killed Lenny's wife.

The pace of the story picks up. Teddy appears at Lenny's car and warns him not to trust Natalie, that Lenny's 'business' in town is done and he should leave. Teddy asks Lenny how he got the car he's driving, the clothes he's wearing? Teddy tells Lenny that Natalie's boyfriend is a drug dealer. Again the next set of questions is being framed for the audience.

Teddy, to Lenny, "You do not know who you are; just who you used to be." This is when Lenny writes on Teddy's photo, "Don't believe him."

We then go back to a scene in Natalie's house. Dodd is someone who's being sent after Natalie because Jimmy disappeared after going to meet Teddy for a drug deal. Natalie wants Lenny to kill Dodd. To give him a reason to do that, Natalie provokes Lenny to hit her. She even tells him, "I'm going to use you." After Lenny splits her lips and blackens her eye, she leaves her house and sits in her car. Lenny frantically tries to find a pen to write himself a note about what's happening, but Natalie has removed all the pens and pencils. When she returns to the house with her split lip, she's able to convince Lenny that Dodd beat her up. This is a powerful story twist, changing entirely the audience's perception of why Natalie is helping Lenny.

We continue back in time to the moment Lenny drives up to the bar where Natalie works in Jimmy's car, and Natalie thinks he's Jimmy. She asks him if he's Teddy, and what happened to Jimmy?

As the story continues to go backwards, we discover that Teddy's is an undercover cop, James Gamol. That Teddy set up Lenny to believe that Jimmy was the drug dealer who murdered his wife.

We then go back to Lenny confronting Jimmy about killing his wife, and Lenny killing Jimmy and putting his body in the basement. This answers a question from the opening scene, the 'truth' that Teddy referred to. Lenny puts on Jimmy's clothes and takes his car. This sets out why Natalie thought Lenny was Jimmy. It also explains why Natalie set Lenny up to kill Teddy, to avenge Jimmy's death. It's a great story twist.

Teddy tells Lenny that Lenny killed his wife, that he simply made up the story about Sammy Jenkins to explain his overdosing his wife with insulin.

That Teddy made up the story of John G. killing Lenny's wife to give Lenny's life meaning. That Teddy already helped Lenny track down the killer and take his life. Somewhere in all this is the truth. Or not. Teddy, "You made up your own truth."

Lenny gets into Jimmy's car with money and a gun from the drug deal.

In the story's final moment, Lenny thinks, "I have to believe my actions still have meaning—that when my eyes are closed, the world's still here."

Like most people, Lenny needs something to believe in.

One of Lenny's last thoughts, "Now, where was I?"

The audience has been shown the answer to that question. Great storytelling.

Chapter Questions

Do you understand the dramatic purpose of each of your scenes?

Do you see what would be missing from your story if you removed any one scene?

Do you understand how to begin a story, introduce its promise, and go back in time to fulfill that promise?

Throwing Your Characters Over the Edge -- Setting Out What's at Stake in Your Stories

Reviews of The Sweet Hereafter, The Five Senses, and Last Night

---

The Sweet Hereafter, novel by Russell Banks, script and direction, Atom Egoyan. Released 1997. Last Night. Written and directed by Don McKeller. Released 1998. The Five Senses. Written and directed by Jeremy Pedeswa. Released 1999. All available on video.

When a story's events shatters the lives of its characters, those characters are thrown over the edge into new worlds. They become dramatic characters because the choices that face them are stark: how will they, can they, survive in these new worlds? How will they change? Can they avoid changing?

In the last year, several movies found different ways to throw characters over the edge: The Sweet Hereafter[38], The Five Senses[39], and Last Night[40].

The Sweet Hereafter begins with a man, woman and baby girl sleeping in an idyllic setting. This quiet, peaceful opening begins a story about loss, by starting with a scene that suggests the opposite, a loving, fulfilling moment in life.

We then cut to Mr. Stevens, played by Ian Holm, a lawyer, who takes a call from his estranged daughter. She's a drug addict and also, we later learn, the baby in the first scene. Because of her drug addiction, he has 'lost' his daughter even though she's alive.

We go from Mr. Stevens, to a father watching his teenage daughter, Nicole, getting ready to perform at a country fair.

Each of these scenes takes place at a different time, but each carries embedded meaning that serves the dramatic purpose of the story. The chronology of the events of any story is not linear. A storyteller chooses those moments in time that best evoke a story's journey.

Mr. Stevens arrives in a small Canadian town as a lawyer seeking to represent the parents of children who died in a tragic bus accident. Because he's tormented over the loss of his daughter, he's focused his life on using others to prove that someone is at fault for every tragedy, that every tragedy has a root cause that can be known and understood. He says to a potential client, "You're angry, aren't you? That's why I'm here. To give your anger a voice. To be your weapon against whoever caused that bus to go off the road."

As we learn more about each parent and the children involved in the accident, the scenes that lead up to the accident develop more and more dramatic power. But when the accident finally happens, we see very little of it. What we see is the shocked look on a father's face as he watches the accident unfold, then later sees a blanket put over the bodies of his dead children.

Then he looks up and sees his children laughing, running toward him in the snow. At the moment of their deaths, they are more alive to him than ever.

Later, as he looks at the hulk of the bus after the accident, he hears the screams of the trapped children. This is a motif that recurs several times.

The loss for Nicole's father is not that she ends up in a wheelchair, but that he loses his dream of helping her become a rock star, a dream he wants to share with her in an intimate way.

As the story advances, one thread occurs years later. On a plane, Mr. Stevens finds himself sitting next to a young woman who his daughter's childhood friend. This brings us to a revelation of what happened in that opening scene. In that idyllic bed a hidden menace struck; baby black widow spiders bit the baby girl. As she began to swell, there is a long ride to the hospital.

during which Mr. Stevens holds his daughter in his lap, a knife ready to cut into her throat if she can no longer breath. Was this the turning point that turned his daughter against him? He can't know, only wonder and grieve.

The story turns when Nicole is asked to testify at a deposition. When she balks, Mr. Stevens tries to manipulate her by telling her that people feel sorry for her because she's in a wheel chair, and testifying is her chance to be angry and get revenge.

She appears ready to go along, but instead, she lies at the deposition, and there is no longer the basis of a law suit against the town or bus manufacturer.

Nicole's reason for lying is set out by her voice over recital of the Pied Piper, in part, "One was lame and could not dance the whole of the way/and after years, if you would blame his sadness/he was used to say/it's dull in our town since my playmates left/I can't forget that I'm bereft/of all the pleasant sights they see/which the piper also promised me/for he led us he said/to a joyus land…where waters gushed and fruit trees grew…and everything was strange and new."

Nicole has left behind the world she once knew. As she narrates at the end of the story, about Ian, "I wonder if you understand, that all of us, Delores, me, the children who survived, the children who didn't, that we're all citizens of a different town now. A place with its own special rules and its own special laws. A town of people living in the sweet hereafter."

Unlike many films, the Sweet Hereafter does not suggest grief and loss can be resolved. It only suggests that life goes on for the grieving, and that we all grieve in our own way, in new worlds created by grief.

A beautiful film.

Another recent film, Last Night, uses a great device to throw its characters over the edge: it's the end of the world; it's happening at a clearly defined moment; no one will be spared.

Each character in the story reacts to this situation according to what's important to them. Some simply want to gather with family like it's a Christmas dinner and pretend all is well. Others riot. Another character arranges to have sex with every woman he's ever had a fantasy about, including his high school English teacher. Another man spends his last hours calling people to let them know the local gas utility has appreciated their patronage.

The story's main character, a young man, wants to die alone. The natural question, why? Fate brings him together with a young woman desperately trying to find her way home to a waiting lover. This also naturally raises a question, why her desperation to get home if the world is ending?

He tries to help her, because helping her means he can die alone. But fate keeps bringing her back. And as the time draws near the end, we find out why he wants to die alone: the loss of his wife who taught him about love has left him bereft. He doesn't want to go through that loss again. Then it comes out why she's so determined to go home: she doesn't want to die a death at the hands of a common fate; she and her lover have made a suicide pact.

She asks him if he'll kill her. The catch is, she needs to fall in love with him to go through with her plan.

He doesn't want to get this involved, but the story ends with the two of them facing each other, guns pointed at the head of the other. But instead of killing each other as the world ends, they do something else that acts out what each was really looking for, what each really wanted to share with someone else.

This story raises a question that has stayed with me, what would I do if the world were coming to an end in the next 24 hours?

A lovely film.

The Five Senses has a plot that revolves around a missing little girl. The mother of the young girl blames a masseuse whose daughter was supposed to be watching the little girl. The mother's feelings of grief, loss and anger are deeply felt.

There are many beautiful scenes in this film, but several stand out. In one, a young man begs the masseuse for a massage. The masseuse at first refuses, then gives in. During the massage, the young man begins to cry. The only time he's touched is when he pays for a massage. Something in his life has thrown him over the edge, outside of normal human contact, and he craves being touched.

Another character is a doctor who eavesdrops on the conversations of others in the office building. The natural question, why? It comes out that he's going deaf and he's trying to store as many auditory sensations as he can. After he admits his situation to someone, he's taken to a concert and shown that he can 'listen' to the music by feeling its vibration on church pews. This moment allows him to feel he can survive in what to him would be the most barren of all worlds, one without sound.

In a turning point, the mother of the missing girl accepts the masseuse in her life as someone who understands how she feels. The lost girl is found, and what else is found is the relationship that had been lost between the masseuse and her teenage daughter.

This is a beautifully told story about how we perceive the world through the senses, and through the memories of our sense experiences.

One way to discover what drives a character is to ask, what is the one thing a character would miss the most if he or her were to lose everything? What a character craves most in life might be a commitment to the truth, a loving relationship, a sense of justice. Throw that character over the edge into a world where what they value most is taken away from them, and that character must react.

Another way to frame this question, what is most important to YOU, the reader, in life? Create a character who loses that, and you can explore your own feelings and thoughts to understand what drives your character to act, to gain some goal, to discover how to exist in the new world you've created.

Chapter Questions

How do you put your characters into situations they must resolve?
How do you put your characters into worlds unknown to them?
If you've ever lost everything in life, are you creating characters who experience the same depth of pain and feeling you felt?

Conclusion: Thoughts on the Craft of Storytelling

Few things in life seem to bedevil so many as this desire to create stories. Just about everyone appreciates a good story. Many try their hand at creating them. Most struggle with rejection or limited success. Or the sense that somehow what they've written isn't generating the same excitement they felt when they created their stories. This book was created to help those who've struggled with the craft of storytelling—to see it not as a mystery with success reserved only for a few, but to show that there are steps in this process of storytelling that can be learned.

Is this book, then, the sure road to fame and fortune as a writer? I've found that worldly success as a writer entails more than writing talent. It requires perserverance in the face of rejection, a business sense, an ability to develop relationships, a singular focus on artistic goals, and an ability to create luck and act on it when it comes around. More likely, for most people, this book offers understanding of the craft of storytelling, and a deeper sense of how to bring stories to life. My wish, that that understanding brings you joy.

A final thought: Perhaps some day on this road of life we'll meet and share a dramatic story or two.

That would be a good ending to the beginning offered in this book.

APPENDIX

Story Questions

CHAPTER ONE

What needs do stories fulfill in your life?

How are the stories you tell yourself about who you are different from your experiences in life?

What needs do the stories you create promise to fulfill for others?

What kind of stories about who you are as a person have been assigned to you by your cultural background? Your income level? Your level of education? Your family background?

Do the stories you enjoy most validate your choices in life? Or do they help you to believe that under different circumstances, you would be a different person?

CHAPTER TWO

What does your story promise its audience?

How do you introduce your story's promise?

What events fulfill your story's promise?

What is the promise of your life story? How does that impact the stories you enjoy?

What details evoke the drama of your story's promise?

CHAPTER THREE

What kind of events or actions or dialogue *names* your story's promise in its opening scenes?

What did you do to create drama around the introduction of your story's promise?

How do the actions of your main characters revolve around resolving your story's promise?

How do the events of your story highlight your story's promise?

CHAPTER FOUR

Can you describe a story line for your story in simple terms and in three sentences?

Can you describe your plot line using three sentences?

Was your first attempt to write something with a story line and plot line obvious and clumsy? Good! Once you learn how to clearly set out your story line and plot line, you can work on creating dramatic beginnings for your stories that are suggestive and dramatic, without being too obscure or too obvious.

CHAPTER FIVE

How are you making a down payment on your story's promise in your opening scenes?

How does your initial down payment draw your audience deeper into your story?

How are you setting up a story question in your opening scenes so that it will draw your audience to the end of your story?

CHAPTER SIX

Describe the beginning, middle, and end of a dramatic moment from the opening scene of your story.

What did you do to make the outcome of that opening moment dramatic?

What information did you offer in that moment that names your story's promise?

How does the dramatic outcome of your opening moment set your plot into motion?

CHAPTER SEVEN

Can you write a sentence that makes a statement about a dramatic truth, and then rewrite it as a sentence that creates an anticipation of a potential outcome for that truth?

Can you write a sentence that vividly expresses the promise of your story?

Can you write a sentence about a character that sets up an anticipation of an outcome for an issue such as courage, self-respect, gaining understanding?

What is the dramatic truth of your life? Are you comfortable with the choices you've made to resolve your dramatic truth?

CHAPTER EIGHT

What dramatic issue most appeals to you in stories?

How do the stories you enjoy most move their core dramatic issue toward resolution?

Can you create premises—in your own words—for some of your favorite stories?

CHAPTER NINE

How does your premise act out your story's promise in an active voice?

How does the goal that your main character seeks to resolve move your story toward its fulfillment?

How does your premise describe your story's fulfillment?

CHAPTER TEN

Who are some of your favorite story characters? Why?

How are some of your characters similar to your favorite story characters?

What are you favorite story characters able to accomplish that you struggle with in life?

When 9/11 happened, did you imagine yourself to be a story character involved in stopping the attack? A rescuer? Did being that character help you deal with your feelings?

Are you allowing your story characters to be larger than life, to resolve issues that you struggle with?

CHAPTER ELEVEN

How does your plot escalate the drama around your story's course and outcome?

How does your plot operate to give your characters a clear dramatic purpose?

How does your plot make your story's fulfillment dramatic?

How do the events of your plot name your story?

CHAPTER TWELVE

How do the events of your plot operate to block the movement of your story?

How does your plot operate to escalate the drama over the course of your story?

How does your plot operate to escalate the drama over the outcome of your story's promise?

CHAPTER THIRTEEN

What's at stake in your story?

What's at stake for the main character in your story?

What's at stake for the character who opposes your main character?

How do you resolve what's at stake in your story?

What events make it clear what's at stake for your main character?

What events make it clear what's at stake for the character who opposes your main character?

What events operate to escalate the drama around the outcome of what's at stake in your story?

What events make visible the resolution and fulfillment of what's at stake in your story?

CHAPTER FOURTEEN

Why are your characters willing to engage in conflict to shape the outcome of your story?

What events in your story block your characters from achieving their goals?

Describe the conflict around your characters shaping the outcome of your story's promise.

CHAPTER FIFTEEN

What conflict is inherent in your story's promise?

How do you introduce the conflict at the heart of your story?

How do the goals of your main character put him or her into conflict with the other characters in your story or with himself or herself?

Can you describe the conflict at the heart of your favorite story?

Can you describe the conflict at the heart of your life?

Can you see how your conflicts in life affect what kinds of stories are more emotionally or thoughtfully engaging for you?

CHAPTER SIXTEEN

What do you consider to be the central idea of your story?

How do you introduce the central idea of your story in a dramatic way?

How do the characters of your story embody its ideas?

What would you say is the central idea that embodies your life? Your needs in life?

How does that central idea or those needs impact the types of story ideas you find engaging?

What story ideas affirm your ideas about life?

What story ideas challenge your ideas about life?

CHAPTER SEVENTEEN

How does the action of the opening scenes of your story serve to thrust your story forward?

What counter-thrust blocks your story's initial forward advance?

Why do your characters persevere when they are blocked?

CHAPTER EIGHTEEN

Write a scene with two characters who say something concrete about their dramatic truths in five words or less. Write five exchanges of dialogue, with each character saying something to the other and their dramatic truth.

Write a scene with two characters who express anger. Write five exchanges. Keep each expression under ten words.

Create characters who have opposing dramatic truths, and put them into a situation where both characters want something, but only want person can leave that room with want they both desire.

Write a scene with five exchanges of dialogue. Have two characters interrupt each other and not allow the other to finish a thought because each is so excited about what they are talking about.

CHAPTER NINETEEN

Without mentioning your characters, can you write a simple story line for your story?

Can you write a simple plot line?

How do the events of your plot compel your characters to speak deeper truths abut themselves, to offer more potent revelations that resonate with your audience?

Do you understand now how your characters advance your story along your story line?

CHAPTER TWENTY

Can you write a story line in three simple sentences for your favorite story?

Can you write a plot line in three sentences for your favorite story?

If this was a struggle for you, were you trying to talk about the events of the story when you wrote a simple story and plot line?

CHAPTER TWENTY-ONE

Did creating the diagram help you see how your story line and plot line work together?

Did it help you see the process of thrust/counter-thrust in your story?

Did it help you to see how your story line and plot line should interweave?

Do you need a larger drawing surface? Some people lay out butcher paper over the top of a table or counter, or tack it up against a wall so they can see the progression of a story and add notes as they have new ideas. Use the outline system that helps you the most. Use none if you feel they intefere with your writing process.

CHAPTER TWENTY-TWO

Are you beginning your story spine with a dramatically interesting sentence that sets out the role of your main character in acting out your story, and a suggestion of what's at stake for that character?

As you write the story spine, are you referring the events of the story to your story's promise in a way that creates a clearly identifiable spine for your story?

Does your synopsis read well? Is it fresh, engaging, dynamic? Does your synopsis clearly suggest what's at stake in the world of your story, and build dramatically from beginning to end?

CHAPTER TWENTY-THREE

What common mistakes of story structure have you made?

How would you correct some of those problems?

Are you using the opening scenes of your story to make statements about who your characters are?

Do your characters embody clearly defined dramatic truths?

Are you exploring the truth of your story through the details you offer about your characters and the environment of your story?

CHAPTER TWENTY-FOUR

Can you write a first sentence for your story that introduces your main character, suggests a dramatic issue, and raises a question that will draw your audience forward to read a second sentence?

Can you follow that with a second sentence that answers a question raised in the first sentence, while raising a dramatic question that will be answered in a third sentence?

Can you keep going and write enough dramatic, lively, engaging, interesting sentences to complete your novel, screenplay, or play?

CHAPTER TWENTY-FIVE

If you were to start a story without an outline, what story idea would you choose to be your compass?

How would you introduce that story idea in your opening scenes?

How would you sustain that idea during the course of your story?

CHAPTER TWENTY-SIX

Can you write a wonderfully clever, dramatic, engaging first sentence for your story?

Do you understand now how this sentence expresses something about the truth of your story? About the promise of your story?

Now write a second sentence that continues to dramatically explore the truth suggested by the first sentence.

Can you keep going until you've finished your novel, screenplay, or play?

CHAPTER TWENTY-SEVEN

How do you introduce your story in a way that both suggests your story's dramatic purpose and creates a mystery around its outcome?

How do you create a plot revelation at your story's climax that is surprising to your audience?

How does your surprise plot climax fulfill your story's premise?

CHAPTER TWENTY-EIGHT

How does your story operate to help your audience transcend ordinary feelings?

What stories help you feel you transcend ordinary life?

How do you structure your story to trigger a transcendent experience for your audience?

CHAPTER TWENTY-NINE

In what way do you give your story a sense of dramatic passion that will engage the interest of your audience?

In what ways do your characters speak with passion about their feelings?

In what way does your story create a richness of feelings similar to those expressed in this play?

When you read your stories, do you feel emotionally moved and thoughtfully engaged?

When your characters are in dramatic, desperate situations, do you feel caught up in the drama you've created?

CHAPTER THIRTY

How do you introduce what's at stake in your story as a story question?

How do you introduce this question in a way that ensures your audience will care about the outcome?

How does your plot operate to increase the dramatic pressure on both your characters and your audience?

How does the plot of your story force your characters into a territory of new feelings and new truths about themselves?

CHAPTER THIRTY-ONE

Is the promise and dramatic purpose of your novel clear from its opening pages, scenes, and first chapter?

Do your opening scenes both introduce your story and set it into motion along its story line and plot line?

What are you doing to create a sense of narrative tension around the actions of your main character?

What are you doing to help transfer that narrative tension from your main character to your audience?

CHAPTER THIRTY-TWO

What questions about the meaning of life does your story raise?

What illuminations about life does your story offer?

How does your story take on a depth of dramatic purpose as it advances?

Do you see the characters in your stories as reflections of you? If so, how does that affect what kind of stories you write?

Do you ever want to become a character in your stories? Why, or why not?

Chapter Thirty-Three

What dramatic truths do your characters embody?

How do they resolve those truths? Fulfill them?

Chapter Thirty-Four

Do you understand the dramatic purpose of each of your scenes?

Do you see what would be missing from your story if you removed any scene?

Do you understand how to begin a story, introduce its promise, and go back in time to fulfill that promise?

Chapter Thirty-Five

How do you put your characters into situations they must resolve?

How do you put your characters into worlds unknown to them?

If you've ever lost everything in life, are you creating characters who experience the same depth of pain and feeling you felt?

Contact Information

Essays, movie reviews, and information about on-line classes by Bill Johnson are available at www.storyispromise.com

Story analysis, editorial consultations, personal consultations, workshops and presentations at writing conferences are also available by writing, calling, or emailing:

Bill Johnson Script Consulting
318 SW Palatine Hill Rd.
Portland, OR 97219
503-452-4778
bjscript@teleport.com

Good luck with your writing!

Resources

BOOKS ON FICTION

Lajos Egri's *The Art of Dramatic Writing!* How to choose and create a pivotal character. Provides an understanding the unity of opposites as a way of perceiving characters who will feel compelled to act in a dynamic way. Explores the role of crisis, conflict, and resolution in a story.

The Elements of Style, by William Stunk and E. B. White. Great introduction to the art of writing in a clear, concise, and active voice.

If You Want to Write: A Book About Art, Independence and Spirit, by Brenda Ueland. (Also available on audio tape). Ueland writes with a rare, forceful spirit about writing with passion and feeling.

The Novelist's Tool Kit, by Elizabeth Lyon. Elizabeth's book is clear, direct, and laid out in an easy to follow manner. Her Compass Series is coming out through Perigee, *A Writer's Guide to Nonfiction* (March '03), *A Writer's Guide to Fiction* ('04), and *A Writer's Guide to Editing and Revision*.

RESOURCE BOOKS:

Insider's Guide to Book Editors, Publishers and Literary Agents, by Jeff Herman. An informative book that offers detailed information about editors and agents. Find out what agents and editors like to read to have a better guide for submitting manuscripts.

Writer's Guide to Software Developers, Electronic Publishers, and Agents, by Sydney Harriet, Ph.D. This book is a good introduction to this new area of writing.

Books by Writer's Digest: *Guide to Literary Agents*. This book is a good guide to agents that is updated yearly. *The Writer's Digest Guide to Manuscript Formats*. This book offers useful tips on preparing query letters, novel manuscripts, proposals, screenplays, and other formats for writing.

Writer's Market. A resource directory updated every year, with information about publishers, magazines, screenwriting, playwriting, general information on writing.

Literary Market Place, R.W. Boker, is the industry guide to the writing industry. Published yearly, it offers information about publishers, agents, and others involved in the world of books and publishing.

Stage Writers Handbook, by Dana Singer. This book is aimed at the world of theatre, but the issues covered—copyright, contract, public domain, etc.—offer useful information to all writers.

BOOKS ON SCREENWRITING

Writing Your Screenplay and*Selling Your Screenplay*, by Cynthia Whitcomb. Two books on screenwriting by a screenwriter who has sold 70 scripts, had 30 produced, and taught screenwriting at UCLA.

Reel Therapy, by Dr. Gary Solomon, reviews over 200 movies that cover such topics as alcoholism, abuse, mental illness, recovery, obsession, etc. This book serves as a well-written reference to movies about dealing with difficult life issues.

WEB SITES ON WRITING

The Screenwriter's Utopia, www.screenwritersutopia.com, is a great new site for screenwriters. The site offers interviews, newsletters, and up-to-date information.

Internet Movie Data Base, www.imdb, offers a wealth of information about writers, casts, directors, and producers.

The Publishing Law Center, www.publaw.com, has articles on legal issues of concern to publishers, editors, and authors. These articles cover contracts, copyright, fair use, public domain, subsidiary rights, electronic rights, and more.

Creative Screenwriting, www.creativescreenwriting.com. This web site features articles from the Creative Screenwriting magazine.

Screentalk, the International Magazine of Screenwriting, www.screentalk.biz. Several of the movies reviewed in this book first appeared as articles in this screenwriting magazine. Great resources for screenwriters.

A Story is a Promise, www.storyispromise.com, my personal web site.

End Notes

[1] I was introduced to the concept of mattering as a story issue by story analyst David Morgan.

[2] This chapter was written and edited in part with the assistance of Lawrence Booth, Founder/Director of the internationally known Film School of Half Moon Bay.

[3] *Rocky*. Written by Sylvester Stallone. Directed by John G. Avildsen.

[4] *The Wizard of Oz*, by L. Frank Baum. William Morrow and Company. ISBN 0688069444

[5] I learned to make this distinction in a class taught by David Morgan.

[6] *The Usual Suspects*. Written by Christopher McQuarrie. Directed by Brian Singer.

[7] *The Hunt for Red October*, by Tom Clancy. Berkley. ISBN 0425133516.

[8] *Moby Dick*, by Herman Melville. Bantam Classic and Loveswept. ISBN 0553213113.

[9] *Prince of Tides*, by Pat Conroy. Bantam Books. ISBN 0553268880.

[10] Funerals for Horses, by Catherine Ryan Hyde. Russian Hill Press. ISBN 0-9653524-3-9.

[11] A Confederacy of Dunces, by John Kennedy O'Toole. Wings Books. ISBN 0-517-12270-7.

[12] From the Corner of His Eyes, by Dean Koonce. Bantam Books ISBN: 0553582747.

[13] *The Art of Dramatic Writing*, by Lajos Egri. Simon and Schuster (paper). ISBN 0671213326.

[14] *Raiders of the Lost Ark*. Conceived by Steven Spielberg and George Lucas, with Andy Kaufman; scripted by Lawrence Kasdan.

[15] *L.A. Confidential*. Based on a novel by James Ellroy; screen credit, Brian Helgeland. Directed by Curtis Hanson.

[16] *The Sixth Sense*. N. Night Shyamalan, writer/director.

[17] Speed. Written by Graham Yost; directed, Jan De Bont.

[18] The Limey. Written by Lem Dobbs, directed by Steven Soderberg.

[19] *The Winslow Boy*. Play by Terence Rattigan. Directed by David Mamet.

[20] *Star Wars*. Conceived and directed by George Lucas.

[21] *Die Hard*. Novel by Roderick Thorp, script by Jeb Stuart. Directed by John McTiernan.

[22] *Honey, I Shrunk the Kids*. Story by Stuart Gordon, script by Tom Schulman.

[23] *Batman Forever*. Story and screenplay by Lee Batchler and Janet Scott Batchler. Directed by Joel Schumacher.

[24] *Lethal Weapon*. Screenplay by Shane Black. Directed by Richard Donner.

[25] *Animal Farm: A Fairy Story*, by George Orwell. New American Library (paperback). ISBN 0451526341.

[26] *The Exorcist*, by William Blatty. Last reprinted by Harper Mass Market Paperbacks. ISBN 0553270109. Available on audio cassette.

[27] *The Accidental Tourist*, by Anne Tyler. Berkley Publishing. ISBN: 9994790889.

[28] *The Bad Beginning*, by Lemony Snicket. Harper Collins. ISBN 0-06-440766-7.

[29] *Harry Potter and the Socerer's Stone*, by J.K. Rowling. Scholastic Press. ISBN: 0590353403.

[30] *Reservoir Dogs*. Written and Directed by Quentin Tarantino.

[31] *Last Action Hero*. Writing credits, Zak Penn, story, Adam Leff. Directed by Richard Donner.

[32] *Silence of the Lambs*. Novel by Thomas Harris, screenplay by Ted Tally. Directed by Jonathan Demme.

[33] *Pride and Prejudice*, by Jane Austen. Wordsworth Classics. ISBN 1853260002.

[34] *Screenplay, Foundation of Screenwriting*, by Syd Field. Paperback. Fine Communications. ISBN 156731239X.

[35] *Cold Mountain*, by Charles Frazier. Vintage Books. ISBN 0375700757.

[36] *Spider*. Novel and screenplay by Patrick McGrath. Directed by David Cronenburg.

[37] *The Full Monty*. Written by Simon Beaufoy. Directed by Peter Cattaneo.

[38] *The Sweet Hereafter*. Novel Russell Banks, script/director Atom Egoyan.

[39] *Last Night*. Written and directed by Don McKeller.

[40] *Five Senses*. Written and directed by Jeremy Pedeswa.

Index